Following My Thumb

A Decade of Unabashed Wanderlust

Following My Thumb

A Decade of Unabashed Wanderlust

Gabriel Morris

Winchester, UK
Washington, USA

First published by Soul Rocks Books, 2012
Soul Rocks Books is an imprint of John Hunt Publishing Ltd., Laurel House, Station Approach,
Alresford, Hants, SO24 9JH, UK
office1@o-books.net
www.o-books.com

For distributor details and how to order please visit the 'Ordering' section on our website.

Text copyright: Gabriel Morris 2011

ISBN: 978 1 84694 849 7

A CIP catalogue record for this book is available from the British Library.

Design: Stuart Davies

Printed in the USA by Edwards Brothers Malloy

We operate a distinctive and ethical publishing philosophy in all
areas of our business, from our global network of authors to
production and worldwide distribution.

CONTENTS

Dedication: to Mom, Dad and Christo…
and to everyone else who tolerated my incessant wandering
(not that I'm finished or anything.)

Foreword

...The beginnings of a hitchhiker

I first started hitchhiking when I was just eight or nine years old. My parents were hippies in the '70s and '80s and we lived up a dirt road outside a small town in rural northern California. The school bus would take me five miles up a winding road and then drop me off at the bottom of our dusty dirt road. From there it was a mile-and-a-half walk to our big cabin in the middle of the woods. For my short legs, following a long day at school, this seemed at times like an impossible trek.

But of course my dad thought it would build character (and thirty years later, I'll admit it probably did) and my whimpering went unheeded. So what if there were a few hills to climb after a long day at school? When my dad was a kid, he'd biked halfway across Los Angeles to go to a school outside of his district, because he played trumpet in their band. At least I didn't have to dodge noisy city traffic and breathe exhaust fumes along the way, and then try to play a trumpet in tune. I was lucky to have clean mountain air to breathe and the soothing sounds of nature to accompany my stroll.

So I trudged reluctantly home each day, creating little mind games to help keep me going. I'd pretend I was on an explorer's expedition in a foreign land, searching for some kind of treasure—maybe a coin or a shiny hubcap or even a Native American arrowhead. Or else I would pick a spot a way down the road and tell myself that all I had to do was make it that far. When I'd made it to that spot, I would pick a spot down the road and keep going, one short, boyish step at a time.

One day, while walking home with my head down, halfway there and wondering if I was really going to make it this time or maybe end up curling up in the woods to take a nap, a car came along and pulled up beside me. Occasionally I would get a ride, if my mom or dad happened to be coming home from work or if one of our immediate neighbors cruised by. I lifted my head in expectation as the man rolled down his passenger window.

"Hey kid, you look beat—you want a ride? I'm going on up the road to see Richard."

I didn't recognize him. He wasn't one of our neighbors or anyone I'd seen before. I considered hopping in, but then remembered my mom's caution about accepting rides from strangers. Well, he *knew* someone I knew. Richard was a friend of my dad's. But he was still technically a stranger, if a friendly one.

"Uh, no thanks," I said. "I'm not going much further." Only another long, hot, blistering mile or so.

"Alright kiddo, no problem—see ya later…" He continued down the road, leaving me in a cloud of dust.

This set me to thinking. I was really tired of walking all the way home every day after school. A quarter-mile would have been fine. Down our long driveway after a ride up the road was no problem at all. But a mile-and-a-half felt, at that moment at least, like cruel and unusual punishment. I wasn't going to do it. I wanted a ride, and I was willing to wait for it. I had a good book in my school backpack, so I sat down under a tree beside the road and started reading. It was warm and sunny and I was immediately happy not to be walking. I loved reading, so suddenly I was doing something that I loved, rather than hated. Why hadn't I thought of this earlier? I felt like that guy must have when he invented shoelaces—something so simple and obvious, yet brilliantly useful. Maybe this wouldn't make me rich. But it would definitely improve my ease of living. I reasoned that I could accept a ride from any person or car I recognized and thus wasn't a complete stranger. Expanding the criterion beyond our immediate neighbors and family friends opened up the possibilities, since dozens of people lived down our road and my family knew most of them to some degree or another. After reading for a half-hour or so, a rusty old Toyota station wagon came clunking along towards me, trailed by the usual roiling cloud of dust. I recognized the car, although I wasn't quite sure who owned it. So I stood up and stuck out my thumb, just like I'd seen older guys doing while on family road trips. The car pulled over. It was a neighbor who lived a little ways past us. His was a familiar face—good enough. I hopped in and got a ride the rest of the way to the top of our driveway.

The following day after the bus had dropped me off, I walked a quarter-mile up the gravel road, sat down in a sunny patch of grass and started reading. When the first familiar car came along, I didn't even get up. I just looked up from my book and held my thumb up high. The car pulled over. It was official—I was a hitchhiker.

Part 1

Europe, 1990

Chapter 1

When in doubt, act like you know what you're doing
(May 1990)

I landed in London, England two days after my eighteenth birthday for a summer abroad; and soon found myself hit by an undeniable wave of culture shock. Other than having lived in Vancouver, Canada for the first year-and-a-half of my life I'd never been outside of the U.S. Now, in a mere matter of hours I was rather abruptly dumped six thousand miles away from everyone and everything familiar to me. It was not unlike stepping into an elevator, and then stepping out of it onto a different planet.

I wasn't altogether certain what I was doing there, so far from home. After reading Mark Twain profusely throughout high school, it had just seemed like the adventurous thing to do: go somewhere far, far away—me, my backpack and my thumb—and see what might happen. As is often the case, reality doesn't hit you until you're dumped headlong into the water. And then it's sink or swim.

I now had four months of solo traveling across a vast, unknown continent ahead of me. And not long after stepping off the plane, the thought of it was already freaking me out. I planned to spend the first month or so hitchhiking around the British Isles. The next three months I would traverse mainland Europe by train. At the time, four months alone away from home seemed pretty much like forever.

My dreams of footloose vagabonding had finally come true. But my first day was a traveler's nightmare. I arrived around noon, went through customs and made my way into the city, via the London Underground, to find a completely unanticipated hot and sunny day. Though I was from California and had just left behind a warm day in San Francisco, somehow this was extremely disorienting. Based on everything I'd heard about Britain, I was mentally and physically prepared for clouds, rain, cold and likely all of the above. I had on three warm long-sleeve shirts as I stepped out of the Underground station, my massive pack clinging to my back, the sun glaring down on me and my blinking, bewildered eyes. I felt something like a caveman transported unexpectedly to modern times—totally overwhelmed by the foreign, chaotic cityscape before me, and totally standing out.

I found a nearby bench to relieve myself of my heavy load for a moment. (Speaking of relieving myself, I seriously had to take a piss...but that would have to wait.) I stripped down to a t-shirt and pulled out a fairly useless map of London (so I soon discovered) that I'd snagged from an info booth at the airport. For some reason I was resolute on finding a campground somewhere near the edge of the city, rather than staying at a hostel. I wanted to spread out and organize my travel belongings in my own space, and be able to relax and get a good night's sleep in my own private tent sans the snores of fellow travelers, or worrying too much about being robbed my first night. But due to complications involving the flimsy tourist map, unfamiliarity with the local transportation system and faulty directions on the part of well-meaning Londoners, I didn't find the accursed campground until three or four more runs on the Underground, miles of walking around London in the beaming sun, multiple bus rides literally back and forth, and finally, a $40 taxi ride— and eight hours later. If ever there were a quintessential first day's discombobulating introduction to a strange and foreign land, I'd just lived through it. But hey, at least I'd avoided getting mugged, ripped off or walking in front of a double-decker bus. It was sun-down when finally, thankfully, I was dropped off at the pleasantly verdant lawn of the campground, somewhere on the outskirts of London. I had no idea where I was and I didn't really care. I could finally stop moving, and that was all that mattered. I walked doggedly to the office, paid for a small campsite, set up my tent, crawled into my sleeping bag and promptly fell into a blessed state of slumberment. My dreams were filled with visions of all the many adventurous and challenging experiences that were no doubt yet to come.

My previous hitchhiking experience had been limited to my small town adventures. Other than thumbing up our dirt road as a kid in high school, I'd started hitching the full six miles home whenever I missed the school bus, or else wanted to stay in town late. And once, my best friend Abram and I went on a day trip to the artsy tourist town of Mendocino on the California coast, thirty miles away. That was pretty much it.

Now I was in London, which was on a different scale from rural northern California. And besides, everyone was driving on the opposite side of the road. This meant learning to look the other way when crossing the street, as well as using my left thumb to hitchhike. And my pack was *so* damned heavy. I remember when I first bought it, being so proud of its immensity and all its fancy pockets and zippers, delighted that I had enough room to take along everything I was certain I needed—including four heavy novels that, for some reason, I thought I'd actually get around to reading. At least I could get the thing (barely) up onto my back—let's hit the road! I still had a thing or two (or fifty) to learn about trotting the globe.

I had no idea how to begin hitching out of London. Standing around at any old stoplight didn't seem like the most effective plan. So I got another expensive cab ride from the campground the next morning, and asked the driver to take me to a motorway heading southwest out of London towards Cornwall. He dropped me off near an on-ramp, and assured me that it was headed in the right general direction. I paid the fare and hiked over to the on-ramp, groaning under the weight of my pack, to stick out my (hopefully) fruitful thumb. Problem was, there was no shoulder where I could stand. I found myself basically squeezed up against the guardrail as cars flew by just inches away from my outstretched arm. And in addition to risking my young life I felt, once again, totally out of place. Though I was somewhere at the edge of London, I was still in the midst of the frenzied, bustling city—a phenomenon I'd experienced only fleetingly, when I moved with my dad to the Bay Area as a teenager. But I was still basically a country boy. My childhood hometown had literally one stoplight when I was a kid. And yet here I was standing *on* the London motorway, attempting to stop traffic, my frazzled blond hair gleaming in the sun like a neon sign, and a backpack so big it might as well have been a billboard over my head reading "I'm a tourist—run over me". Despite attempting to portray myself as someone who knew what he was doing, I undoubtedly didn't. This was clearly dangerous and naive, and most likely illegal.

I was amazed when, fifteen minutes later, I actually got a ride—and from a lorry driver no less, a big-rig that pulled over and held up traffic while I tackled the daunting task of getting myself and my backpack up into the enormous vehicle. The passenger door swung open as a disembodied voice hollered down at me from far above to hop on in, and make it quick. My pack seemed to double in size, now that I had to lift it not just up to my waist, but up and over my head. The truck's seat was so elevated that I had to hoist my pack, reeling under its weight, onto the upper foot-step at about chest-height, and then crouch down underneath and push it the rest of the way up with my back, head and arms.

By the time I'd actually gotten myself and my pack firmly into the passenger's seat, I was so dazed and worn out by the ordeal that I'd temporarily forgotten I was in a strange land halfway around the world, stuck there on my own for a third of a year. This realization hit me full force as we started up the on-ramp, entered the frenetic congestion of the motorway and then left London behind, headed for Land's End at the tip of Cornwall in south-western England. I began wondering if I was really the adventurous soul I'd first set out as, or if maybe I should just go back home, and sit under a tree.

A couple of hours later though, after chatting with the sociable lorry driver for a while and then sitting back comfortably in my seat high above the rest of the vehicles, listening to Pink Floyd blast through my walkman, watching the pleasant English countryside roll by effortlessly, I was thinking to myself with sheer, unbridled euphoria: "Yeah man, now *this* is what it's all about!"

Chapter 2

Loch Ness, and other mysteries
(May 1990)

A few weeks later, I was trying to hitch a ride out of Aberdeen, Scotland. I was headed towards the village of Inverness on the shores of the legendary Loch Ness. My first hitchhiking adventure abroad was, for all practical purposes, a success. I'd indeed made my way to Land's End, where I stared contemplatively out to sea back towards my home continent, on the other side of virtually infinite waters (otherwise known as "the pond"). I'd hitched through towns big and small, slept in city parks and various other strange places, toured castles and other relics of history and met an assortment of intriguing characters along the way, both locals and fellow travelers.

My overstuffed backpack had lightened considerably since my rather bumbling arrival in the U.K. A week or so after leaving London, as I was preparing to hike to a hostel via a seaside trail along the Cornwall coast, I realized that *The Mists of Avalon*, regrettably, had to go; along with the other weighty books I'd packed other than my travel guide, two of my thick long-sleeved shirts, my felt cowboy hat (wide brims didn't last long on the road, I soon realized) and a few other nonessential items. Not knowing what else to do with it all, I'd bundled the small load up in one of the shirts and hid it underneath a large bush near the trailhead. Then I drew myself a rudimentary map so that I could find it should I ever, for some reason, come back that way again. Either there's an Englishmen in Cornwall now walking around sporting my black felt cowboy hat, or else there's a moldy pile of crap still sitting under that bush.

From there I'd hitched north through central England, visited the quaint university town of Oxford, and headed west into Wales to tour a few of its historic and imposing castles. After several stormy days of rain in Wales, I headed for the remote Lake District of England's north country. There, I met up with a couple of Brits and an Aussie at a hostel, and the three of us explored the pleasant, mystical hills there for much of a week. Then I'd continued hitching north into Scotland.

I wasn't quite sure what I expected to find at Loch Ness. Not the Loch Ness Monster, no doubt. But northern Scotland had a sort of archaic appeal that drew me to investigate. The most intriguing thing it was known for around the world, other than kilts and the plaintive shrill of bagpipes, was a mythical beast, which supposedly lived beneath the surface of a bottomless lake. This was the sort of story that captivated my imagination. I'd always had a strong interest in the paranormal and other-worldly. I was one keen on unraveling life's mysteries—or at least in encountering them. After an hour or so of sitting there at Aberdeen watching the traffic roll by, a car finally pulled over. I got up to see where it was headed. The driver was a kind, middle-aged businessman on his way home to Inverness, a town nestled around the north end of Loch Ness. There was a big, black, hairy, slobbering dog of some sort in the passenger seat, which the driver shoved affectionately into the back. I grabbed my backpack and climbed in, pulling my pack onto my lap.

"So, where ya from, mate, and what brings ya to Scotland?" he asked as we continued down the road.

"United States," I said. "Just traveling around Europe for the summer. Seeing the sights, footloose and all, you know. I'm hitch-hiking around the British Isles first. Then I've got a Eurail train pass for the rest of Europe."

"Ah, flitting about a bit, eh?"

"Sure, I guess you could say that."

"You hopin' to catch a glimpse of ol' Nessie while you're up this way? I hear there was a sightin' not long ago. Some old fishermen say she grabbed his line, and then took off with the pole. Probably just a big fish he couldn't handle—or else the bloke was doused and just lost the thing. It seems every couple of years someone says they seen her. It keeps the tourists a'comin'."

"Well, heck, I certainly wouldn't mind catching a glimpse of the creature—as long I was on shore, of course! That'd sure be a story to take back home. But really, I'm just here to see this part of the country. It sure is a beautiful neck of the woods."

"Aye, that it is…"

After some more small talk, and a little further down the road, he invited me to come over and have supper with both he and his wife. I gladly accepted his invitation, grateful for the hospitality and the chance to get a little taste of the local fare. Soon we showed up at his simple home at the edge of Inverness. His wife came to the door as we all piled out of the car. She seemed remarkably calm about her husband unexpectedly bringing home a foreign traveler after a day's work at the office. She kissed her husband, patted the dog as it galloped into the house and then welcomed me in.

"There's always enough in the cupboards for a guest," she said. "Especially one from so far away! I'll just set another place at the table."

Except that, as it turned out, we didn't eat at the table. Instead they told me to set my pack down by the door, take off my boots and make myself comfortable on the couch. Then they turned on the TV and we all sat around the living room, ate fish and chips and watched Scottish game shows, as they asked me curiously about my travels around Britain the past few weeks. They seemed as interested in hearing about other parts of their own country as I'd been in visiting them. In the past few weeks, I'd glimpsed more of the U.K. than they'd seen first-hand in their lifetimes. Following dinner, the couple invited me to go with them for a walk along nearby Loch Ness. As it was summer in northern Scotland, the evenings were long. They said that, afterwards, they could drop me off at the hostel in town. After digesting our meal to some quirky British sit-coms, we all climbed into the car, including the large, slobbering dog. We drove slowly through the charming tourist town of Inverness; then continued a ways down one side of the vast lake, before pulling over to get out and stretch our legs.

Seeing Loch Ness in person was truly awe-inspiring, even sans the appearance of any magical, watery creatures. The lake is close to twenty-five miles long and almost a mile wide. The water is extremely deep, as well as dark and murky due to an overabundance of peat moss carried along by the many rivers and streams flowing into it. And the surrounding landscape is eerily beautiful, with softly rolling hills and thick, deep green forests. It seemed, indeed, the ideal setting for a monster sighting, or else a fantastical legend of some other sort. It wouldn't have been so out of place for a knight in shining armor to have come bursting headlong out of the woods. But we didn't catch sight of the Loch Ness Monster, or anything else we could have exaggerated as such. I wasn't terribly disappointed, having found more or less what I'd come there for. After our stroll along the water's edge, they took me back into town and dropped me off at the hostel. It was right across the street from a pub, which they highly recommended. I thanked them for their hospitality and kindness, petted the slobbering dog, grabbed my pack and threw it over my shoulder as I waved goodbye. After checking in at the hostel, I wandered over to the pub for a drink and to ponder the mysteries of the universe, monsters and otherwise. I didn't manage to unravel any. But eventually, as the cold and very large mug of beer slowly and surely drained away and my beer buzz correspondingly thickened, my thoughts wandered back to the theme of "what the heck I was doing here".

Although I had just turned eighteen weeks before, I'd actually graduated from high school a year earlier. I'd skipped eighth grade in order to be in the same grade as my best friend, and because my teachers and parents thought I could handle it. Despite that (or perhaps because of it to some extent), my grades throughout high school were somewhat mediocre—other than my last semester of senior year.

My dad came up with an ingenious plan to get my grade point average up a notch and give me a decent chance of at least getting into a state university—he bribed me. He would pay me $100 for every B I got, and $200 for every A. This didn't apply to the two electives I was taking, which I didn't need to graduate. But still, if I got straight A's I could make a cool thousand bucks. I decided to screw the electives, and just focus on the other classes. I pulled off all A's and a B in my core classes, and made 900 dollars. I used that to buy a new computer. The next fall, I moved from the Bay Area back north to my mom's house near the little town where I grew up, and started attending classes at the local community college. It didn't take long however before I was thoroughly bored. I didn't feel like sitting at a desk in a classroom any longer. Twelve years was enough. I'd been reading about other people's exciting travels, fiction and non-fiction for, well, as long as I could read. Mark Twain, J.D. Salinger, Henry Miller, J.R.R. Tolkien, *The Hitchhiker's Guide to the Galaxy*, *Blue Highways*, *Zen and the Art of Motorcycle Maintenance*, and the list could go on for a long, long while. There was a hell of a lot of fun and adventure to be had out there in the wide world, and I was dying to leap into it. The problem was, I was still seventeen. Oh yeah, and I had no money. From the end of that semester, it would have to wait another four months. I told my mom I couldn't stand another semester of community college, and wanted to go to Europe. She conferred with my dad, and I ended up moving back down to Oakland to live with my dad again for the next few months. I got a job scooping ice cream. Then I sold my almost-brand-new computer to my aunt for close to what I'd paid for it. And thanks to a cheap round-trip flight from San Fran to London, once my eighteenth birthday rolled around on the last day of April, I was ready to rock'n'roll.

And so here I was, a long way from the constrictions of a school desk, living the budget traveler's dream. No longer twiddling my thumbs, I was flexing them. And they were taking me places. I'd managed to hitchhike straight out of London; and then followed my thumb all the way to northern Scotland, where I now found myself chugging a pint of beer in a pub on the shores of Loch Ness. I could hardly be farther away from the familiar. The future was altogether unknown. I wasn't sure what I was doing yet tomorrow, or where I would be a month from now. This was both a thrilling state of being, and a disconcerting one.

My future plans beyond this trip and my inevitable return to the home front were equally wide open and murky. I'd only gotten around to applying to one university, the University of Alaska of all places, to their creative writing department. I didn't know yet if I'd been accepted, or how I would pay for it if I was. I'd applied there pretty much on a whim, inspired by that same quest for adventure and something completely different. If that didn't work out, maybe I'd just hit the road again once I got back home, and let me thumb lead the way across the U.S.A. There was a lot of my own country I still had yet to see.

But all that was a long way off. Months, and each week on the road felt like a lifetime in itself. I wasn't going to solve those future quandaries right now, any more than I was going to find the Loch Ness monster swimming about at the bottom of my beer mug. The present moment was the place to be, and I would cross those other bridges once I got to them. All I knew for certain right then, was that a cold pint of beer sure quenched my thirst after another long and winding day on the road.

Chapter 3

Those beautiful Swedish women
(June 1990)

On the long ferry ride from southern Italy over to Greece, I sat down on the outside deck next to an alarmingly beautiful young woman. The boat was crammed with other budget travelers and for some reason it was one of the few available spaces. She was sitting there on the wooden floorboards with her belongings spread out all around her. There was a vacant plastic seat randomly placed nearby, which I thankfully relaxed into as I set down my pack. I relaxed back in my chair, fired up my Walkman and put on the earphones, rocking out to The Doors as we left Italy behind and sailed into the serene Mediterranean and the all-pervading blue, from sea to sky. I was excited to be headed for Greece. For one thing, it was supposed to be cheap compared to the rest of Europe, and my meager budget was being seriously stretched. But more importantly, the sun was rumored to shine on a regular basis there.

I'd spent a month altogether on the eternally overcast (other than my first few days) British Isles. I hitchhiked the entire length of Britain, from Land's End all the way to John'O'Groats at the northernmost point of Scotland. Then I took a ferry over to northern Ireland, where I spent a week doing more sporadic hitchhiking and exploring, crossing the width of Ireland. I started utilizing my Eurail train pass in Dublin (which gave me two months of unlimited train travel across Europe). From Dublin I took the train down to the port of Rosslare in the south and then hopped a ferry over to the western coast of France, at Le Havre. From there I caught another train straight to Paris.

I stayed a week in Paris. I visited several museums, spent

hours wandering the Louvre, clambered up the Eiffel Tower and did lots of aimless wandering through the convoluted maze of city streets. I enjoyed Paris, except that, like the British Isles, it was cloudy or rainy pretty much the whole time I was there. I needed some serious uplifting after the perpetual gray of Britain. I wanted sun, I wanted a tan, I wanted to swim in warm seawaters and drink cold, cheap beer on the beach. I wanted some good, solid hedonistic leisure time after spending 8-12 hours a day on the road hitchhiking the expanses of both Britain and Ireland. I decided on an impulse to head straight for Greece; taking the train from Paris down through Italy, and then hopping on another ferry at the southern port of Brindisi, to sail across the Ionian Sea.

It turned out she was a Doors fan. I was singing, "People are Strange" under my breath with my eyes closed, when I heard her say to me:

"Oh, I love that song—you think I could listen sometime?"

After the song was finished, I handed her the Walkman to listen to for a while. It was a twelve-hour ferry ride and eventually we struck up a conversation. Her name was Johanna, from Sweden, she spoke near-perfect English, and had the sexiest accent I've ever heard. She was also a hardy independent traveler, having been on her own throughout much of Europe, including Czechoslovakia and Yugoslavia. Not easy territory to wander through as a single young female. I definitely had some admiration for these adventurous, daring, travel-worn women (along with a good dose of youthful lust).

Upon disembarking at the port in western Greece, most of the passengers made their way to the nearby train station, to head directly to Athens. Johanna and I meandered slowly through the small Grecian town together on our way over to the station. We bought a small watermelon and some other travel food to share, and then hopped on the waiting train and squeezed into a compartment along with four other young travelers from the ferry. At that point it was about midnight, and we had another long ride through the night ahead of us. None of us felt much like sleeping. Besides, there was nowhere to lie down other than to lean against the wall, or the shoulder of the smelly traveler next to you. So we sliced up the watermelon and passed it around, along with the other snacks, and then carried on random, rambling conversation throughout the late-night hours as the train creaked and swayed along.

We pulled into Athens early the next morning. I didn't have much idea as to where I was going from there. I was just searching for a nice beach to relax on for a while and catch some warm rays. Johanna was heading out to the Greek islands, and invited me to join her. That sounded like as good of an idea as I could possibly come up with. We caught a city bus to the port at Piraeus, getting a brief glimpse of Athens coming to life in the early morning hours. Despite the smog, urban grime and bustling confusion, Athens intrigued me. Such a marked difference from the Europe I'd seen up until then, so far away from the stifling, shrouded gray of Britain and Paris, in many ways. Maybe it was just my own inner hunger for light, and for a change of scene and pace. But the Greek people seemed richer in human presence somehow, more vibrant and active, yet less hurried at the same time, more personable and natural.

It struck me that perhaps the mere presence of the sun inspires the soul to shine a little brighter, bringing out a warmer, more expressive part of the human character. Just pondering the cultural clichés of northern vs. southern Europe, there does seem to be more of a tendency for people to open up and let their humanness and their passions hang out, when that great ball of fire is hovering overhead. Not to be too shallow and insulting, but if there were a contest held pitting the Danes, Fins and Norwegians against the Spaniards, Italians and Greeks for vibrancy of character and passionate expression, would it really be any contest?

Whether it be the sun, or perhaps something emanating from the sea, it was working wonders on me already, slowing me down, easing me more into the moment. I was feeling less focused on a destination, more content with being pretty much right where I was. Although, I knew I'd be even more in the moment, once I was feeling some soft, golden sand between my toes and a cold beer trickling down my throat.

Johanna and I decided to buy a ticket to the first of the Greek islands on the ferry line, Kea, and just check it out, since neither of us had been to Greece before. Besides, my guidebook covering the whole of Europe offered only scant descriptions of a few of the Greek isles (of which there are hundreds). Upon arriving at the dock a few hours later, however, we decided to continue on and see if the next island might better fit our visions of Mediterranean isle paradise. We were in no huge hurry to get off the boat, sailing through calm seas beneath endless blue skies, with each other as company.

When we arrived at the next island, we found ourselves similarly uninspired. So we decided once again to continue on until we came to an island that appeared acceptably idyllic. We had expectations of somewhere steeped in an ambience of exotic and tranquil romanticism, dripping with vivid, colorful Greekness, a world and a few decades apart from modern civilization. In other words, our expectations were unreasonable. But we were young and prone to the notion that if something was in our head, it correspondingly existed somewhere in reality. Finally, four or five more unsatisfactory islands down the line and half a day later, we got off the ferry at the final ferry stop, Santorini, only because we had to. We felt a little guilty for not paying full fare for the ten-hour ferry ride, but not much.

As it turned out, our adolescent imaginings revealed themselves to be not so irrational after all. Santorini proved to be exquisitely beautiful and gloriously enigmatic even beyond our fanciful idealistic concoctions. The ferry docked at a tiny port at the base of sheer, stark black cliffs a thousand feet high, which hovered imposingly over the gentle blue sea. A tiny, tiny dirt road snaked back and forth up the cliff face, barely suspended on the precipice it seemed. Buses carried loads of backpackers up and down, to and from the ferry dock. There were a few strategic wide spots along the way where the buses could barely pull over to pass one another.

We caught the second or third bus. Everyone had gotten off the ferry at that point, leaving an impatient crowd of young travelers clustered together in a dusty parking area. As the next empty bus pulled up, one of the bus-hands jumped off, grabbed our packs abruptly from us and then threw them onto a creaky wooden platform attached to the rear of the bus. Forty or fifty packs were then piled onto the platform and the whole mess was quickly tied down. I wondered if the load had ever given out while going up the steep hill. Fifty backpacks falling elegantly down the cliff face—one of those beautifully tragic images that hung in my mind, as I peered upwards. I'm sure they took the appropriate precautions to avoid this, even if it didn't appear so by how rapidly they loaded up the bus to overflowing capacity, and then were cranking up the precipitous hill.

We rode a half-hour or so to the opposite side of the small island. Santorini was like a huge tilted stump sticking out of the sea, with the steep cliffs on one side, then sloping down to a mellow, sandy shore on the other. Upon consulting our guidebooks, Johanna and I decided to head for the quaint village of Perissa, right near a good beach and with a cheap hostel. I'd ended up doing a lot of camping in northern England and Ireland after exceeding my budget on relatively spendy hostels during my first few weeks of traveling. But in Greece at the time (a decade before the Eurodollar jacked up prices) the hostels were only about three bucks a night. Also, in stark contrast to the stricter rules of hostels in the rest of Europe, here they had co-ed dorms. After getting off the bus in the small seaside village and then finding the hostel, we registered and paid at the front desk. Then Johanna and I claimed two bottom bunks next to one another. We stuffed our backpacks underneath our beds, grabbed our wallets and strolled into town to look for some dinner to fill our hollow bellies.

It had been a whirlwind of traveling the past few days. And I was definitely feeling it. I was starved for a decent meal and an uninterrupted night's sleep. Adding everything up, it had been thirty-six hours by train from Paris to Brindisi, Italy; twelve hours by ferry from Italy over to Greece; another six hours on the train to Athens; and then ten more hours on the ferry out to Santorini. Almost three full days of travel. I could scarcely believe where I now found myself, deposited on a small island in the middle of the Mediterranean, a clear, unbroken blue sky overhead, the lulling sounds of the gentle waves lapping calmly somewhere nearby, the sun sinking slowly into a placid sea. The quaint, unhurried Cycladic island village felt like stepping back in time a good fifty years.

Johanna and I soon found a nice rooftop restaurant overlooking the black sand beach and the lapping waves, and ordered a couple of cold beers to sip while we languished over the menu. I was still adjusting to the concept of being able to legally drink alcohol, since I was under age back home in the States. I still associated drinking a beer with my high school days of being sneaky and unlawful. I did my best to kick back, relax and breathe in the warm evening breeze, now that I'd apparently found the exquisite island paradise I'd been looking forward to since my revelation in Paris, and subsequent impulsive flight from the unrelenting drizzle.

As my beer buzz thickened, and reality began to seep slowly into my tired, travel-worn mind, I found myself drifting into one of those peculiar states of being in which you start to feel as if you're looking out at a panoramic movie screen before you, rather than actually living the scene around you. The woman sitting before me was a vision of beauty, as if she'd just stepped out of a fantasy film in which she reigned over a kingdom of unicorns and fairies. She had long, wavy, sandy-blond hair, a soft, vibrant face with deep, thoughtful brown eyes and was wearing tight shorts over a faded red swimsuit that concealed firm and ample breasts. She was strong, independent and intelligent, yet totally feminine and endlessly alluring. She was pretty much everything I desired in my wildest of romantic juvenile dreams. I'm sure that she would have made an excellent queen of the fairies. I just wasn't certain in that moment that I was prepared to be her knight in shining armor, should that be her expectation. Come to think of it, I wasn't quite sure how I'd ended up sitting there with her at all.

My previous romantic experience with women bordered on nil. As much as I could tell it wasn't due to complete unattractiveness on my part, just timidity and lack of finesse in the matter. My best friend Abram and I had basically been outcast freaks all through high school—bored creative teenagers in a small, redneck town. The 1980s weren't a pretty decade for popular culture to begin with, and so we'd figured that just being all-out weird was a sure way not to fit in and thus distance ourselves from the blandness of top-40 conformity. We'd shaved our eyebrows once in honor of the main character from Pink Floyd's movie *The Wall*; cut class to talk to spirits on a Ouija board; and would laugh hysterically in public over seemingly ordinary things, without taking drugs, simply because we knew the world to be a demented place—and that laughter was ultimately the best medicine.

We hung out with some cool girls. We just never got around to getting involved with any of them, for inexplicable reasons. It was almost as if having a girlfriend was too cliché for us. We didn't want to be like all the other annoying macho jerks in high school, flexing our muscles and bragging about cars, how much we could drink, how tough we were or whatever to impress the

23

women. Granted, Abram and I and our cadre of quasi-nerds had little in the way of muscles, cars, toughness or any of the usual symbols of manliness to work with. I had yet to figure out that sweetness, creativity and a sense of humor might be favorable traits in relating to the opposite sex. Basically, I'd kissed a couple of awkward times, and had some fun female friendships.

So the fact that nothing at all passionate or sensual happened between Johanna and I was, looking back on it, due purely to bumbling naiveté on my part. We hung out together on Santorini for most of a week and had a blissful time exploring the small, tranquil island together. One afternoon we rented a moped between the two of us, then drove together with just our sleeping bags, some bread, cheese and a bottle of wine to a remote black sand beach on the other side of the island. Nobody else was around. We made a campfire in the sand that evening and sat around the flickering fire, talking, sipping slowly on the wine, laughing, enjoying the sounds of the sea waves lapping away nearby, and the half-moon shining down through a thin, moody haze.

Eventually we fell asleep in the sand next to one another, huddling together in our thin sleeping bags in the cool night air. I remember her complaining in the middle of the night of the cold. But I was too shy to reach an arm around and get some physical affection going to warm us both up. In short, I was a damned fool. I could be telling you right now about smooching by moonlight one of the most gorgeous Scandinavian women in the world, at a secluded beach on a remote Mediterranean island. It doesn't get much closer to a young man's whimsical dreams than that.

But sadly, the story is that I wimped out. Oh well, I was only eighteen. That's my feeble excuse. If only you could write the story first and then live the tale, instead of the other way around. Sometimes you don't quite realize the potent, fleeting moment you're experiencing until you look back at it from the distance of a decade or two. And the vision of hindsight is always so much clearer...or so we imagine.

The next morning, after a leisurely swim in the warm, placid sea, we cruised on the moped together back to the hostel. And sometime over the next couple of days, with a friendly goodbye, we simply drifted off into our own separate adventures down the traveler's trail.

Chapter 4

Uniting body and mind
(August 1990)

A month after Santorini, I'd made my way by ferry and train back north through Italy, Austria, Germany and Switzerland. Eventually I wandered into the south of France; where I left the train tracks behind and did some random hitchhiking through the Pyrenees Mountains, skirting the Spanish border. I would have loved to venture into Spain. But I was nearing the end of my four months in Europe and didn't want to stray too far from London, and risk missing my flight back home.

After a long day standing on the side of quiet two-lane roads, not getting very far, I caught a short ride with a French couple and was dropped off in a tiny mountain village. As it was early evening by that time, I cast around for somewhere to spend the night before dark. Due to my rapidly dwindling budget, I was now rarely paying for a place to lay my head. Instead I was counting on my tent and sleeping bag, some concerted resourcefulness and a little luck to help me find somewhere to sleep, whenever possible. Worn out from the long and rather fruitless day of hitching, I got frustrated looking unsuccessfully for a decent spot to set up my tent in the woods outside of town. I trudged back into the center of the village, not quite sure at that point how to solve my sleeping dilemma, part of me not even caring. I just wanted to give my weary body a much-deserved rest.

I sloughed off my pack with a groan next to an old wooden barn, oddly placed near the town center. Then I sat down on my pack to ponder my quandary, leaning back against the wooden wall of the barn. My body thanked me gratuitously for the chance, finally, to take a load off, as I slumped into an exaggerated slouch—despite the fact that soon enough I would have to haul my ass back up and find somewhere to crash for real.

My stomach growled. I pulled some bread and cheese from my pack to placate my inner rumblings. As the sun went down over the nearby hills, the daylight steadily waned. But I just kept sitting there, putting off the inevitable, like when you're warm and cozy under the blankets on a cold morning. It felt far too good, staying right where I was, to bother with moving; though I knew eventually something else would have to happen.

Soon my mind was nagging me worriedly: "Dude, you've got to find us somewhere to sleep, before it gets too dark."

And my tired body answered: "Relax, man, stop stressing it, no worries—just give me a few minutes. I'm all over the finding-a-place-to-crash thing, you'll see."

"What do you mean, all over it?" responded my mind impatiently. "You're just sitting there on your boney rear end, you lazy bum! Now get the heck up and find us somewhere to sleep!"

"Hey, easy enough for you to say. All you have to do is give the command. I've got to actually carry out the action. Hold that thought another minute or two, and I'll get on it when I'm good and ready…"

As I sat there carrying on this ridiculous conversation with myself (my body clearly not getting the job done, or so it seemed), an older man came along down the small lane, leading two young girls and a guy with small rucksacks, all looking roughly high school aged. The old man slid open the large barn door about fifteen feet away from me, and the four of them disappeared inside. A few minutes later, the man came out alone and walked past me down the dusty little road. Another ten or fifteen minutes later, the three young travelers came out— without their rucksacks now—and also walked right past me. I nodded a friendly hello as they passed by. They all said "Bon jour" back—definitely real French.

My mind and body had a spontaneous moment of unity, as they got together on this little parade of events and quickly added everything up, with mutual agreement: One of the three kids was the older man's niece or nephew or grandkid. The other two were school friends traveling with them. The old man owned the barn, and was letting them sleep in it for the night while they passed through town. With this conclusion, all dissent between my mind and body ceased. We, both of us, were spending the night in that barn...That is, assuming we could muster up a bit of luck, and enough composure to be acceptably sociable.

"Now," said my mind to my body, "what's the friendliest face you can come up with?"

About half an hour later, as dusk was clearly settling upon me and I was beginning to wonder if I might just end up sleeping right there against the barn wall, curled up in a ball, the three young folks came wandering by again. They seemed a little perplexed to see me still sitting there against their barn. I glanced up as they neared. As they walked past, I gave a big, warm smile and a "Bon jour" —definitely not real French, but plenty friendly. Once again, they disappeared into the barn. I sat there a little dejected, yet still hopeful.

About ten minutes later one of the girls came out of the barn, walked over to me and said,

"Bonjour—parle vous Francais?"

"Bonjour. No—Anglais," I replied.

"Oh, okay," she said. "What is your name? Where you are from?"

"I'm Gabriel. From America, the U.S."

"I see. Well, I am Angeline, from Paris...We are wondering—you need somewhere to sleep tonight? It's getting dark, and we were thinking we should invite you inside. My uncle owns this barn, and I think he won't mind if you stay here the night, too."

"Hmmm," I mused, trying my best to act casual. "Hey, that's great. Yeah, I do need somewhere to sleep, actually. I was just sitting here, you know, thinking about it—where to sleep for the night."

I got up off my pack and pulled it over my shoulder, as I followed her to the barn door, and we slipped inside.

"See??" said my body to my mind. "I told you I was all over it."

The three young friends were on a week-long high school field trip from Paris. The rest of their group of classmates was camped out with their teachers, near a lake high in the Pyrenees a ways outside of town. They'd hitched into this village by themselves to visit her uncle for the night, as a fun side trip.

Their belongings were spread out on the bales of hay stacked neatly on the upper level of the barn, their sleeping bags laid out on the natural padding. The two girls both spoke fairly good English; the guy spoke just a little. We hung out in the hay, chatting for a while through the evening. They were curious to hear of my travels throughout Europe, and how I'd ended up in this small town in the French Pyrenees—as well as why I'd been leaning against this barn at sunset, of all possible places, instead of getting a room for the night. My answers seemed to satisfy their collective curiosity. Eventually we crawled into our respective sleeping devices, to catch a few winks on the soft hay.

The next morning we packed up our backpacks and shuffled out of the barn into the unhurried Pyrenean village. They invited me to hitchhike with them back up to their camp in the mountains, to meet their fellow schoolmates and teacher. I said sure, why not. I had no major plans, no particular schedule other than a plane to catch in a week or so. We hiked up the road out of town to stick out our thumbs.

We ended up getting a ride on an in-service commercial bus. Other than the driver, nobody else happened to be on it. He was extremely friendly and probably just wanted some company since he didn't have any riders. He happened to be going close to the campground where the rest of the students were all camped. We relaxed back in the empty seats through the next hour of winding, uphill road. He dropped us off at a fork in the road, from where we quickly caught another ride up to the campground.

The campground was at a beautiful, deep blue lake, sandwiched firmly between two spectacular, soaring, snow-capped peaks. Upon walking up to their campsite, the four of us were greeted by two-dozen excited and curious Parisian sixteen-year-olds, asking (so I gathered) about their schoolmates' side trip—as well as who the heck I was. Though I spoke basically no French and most of them spoke limited English, I was whole-heartedly welcomed among them.

I spent the next few days camped out with the French school kids, hiking around the mountains a bit and even taking a very brief dip in the near-freezing lake. Soon I continued on my way. I hitched back down through the Pyrenees along winding mountain roads, passing through more quaint, quiet villages; eventually coming to a train station at a slightly larger town in the foothills of the mountains. I spent that night on the station floor, huddled in my sleeping bag underneath a bench. From there I hopped on a train heading north, once again to Paris.

Chapter 5

Sleep under the bridge, not on it
(August 1990)

I stepped off the train in Paris and, upon contemplating where to stay for a night or two that wouldn't entirely evaporate the contents of my wallet; I realized that I was seriously running out of money. I was flying out of London in less than a week, and had barely enough left in traveler's checks to cover the basic expenses until then. But I wanted some spending money left over so that I could spend a few days exploring London. All I'd seen of it after initially flying in was that first day as a very tired, sweaty and bedraggled virgin foreign traveler with a massive hump clinging to my back. Not the best scenario for taking in the sights.

Hoping to somehow avoid paying for a room that night in Paris, I ended up hanging out at a Burger King for hours, drinking cheap coffee and mulling over my sleeping options, and not coming up with much. Finally I was kicked out of the restaurant when they closed at midnight. Once again, my lack of planning in the sleeping department seemed to be hurling me headlong into an escapade of some sort.

I stood there in front of the Burger King awaiting deliverance from my self-inflicted plight, my backpack clenching my back as usual, like distressed offspring. As I was looking up and down the street, pondering where I could possibly lay out my sleeping bag in the middle of Paris where I wouldn't be robbed or worse — perhaps under another bench at the train station as a last resort — a man walked up to me and said, in a thick Italian accent:

"Hello, friend — you need place for sleeping?"

I was in the midst of contemplating a response to his question since it wasn't precisely a yes or a no, when he continued walking up the sidewalk with a friendly wave of his hand, saying "Come, you stay with me, no problem." (I'll have to keep in mind that whenever an over-friendly stranger in a foreign country says "no problem", that means there's going to be a problem.)

Having little else in mind as a solution to my sleeping dilemma, I decided to walk along with him and at least converse a bit. Hopefully I'd pick up a clue as to his motivation for being helpful. Otherwise, I would simply go with plan B, which I was still planning, but would undoubtedly muster up in the nick of time. Necessity is the mother of invention, after all. Hopefully all that crappy coffee would at least help fuel a revelation.

His English was minimal, so I had a hard time understanding him as we wandered down the empty streets of Paris. He had the usual lively and animated Italian manner of expression (which I knew well enough, as my grandfather was full-blooded Italian). He kept making these wild gestures with his hands as he spoke in a jumbled mixture of English, Italian and French, trying to fill in the missing spaces with sign language. Eventually I got the basic message, that he worked in a nearby restaurant and was on his way home, and that he would put me up at his place in exchange for something. I just wasn't quite clear as to what the "something" was.

I knew, of course, that I probably shouldn't consider spending the night with a stranger under these circumstances—in a big city, having met the stranger late at night outside of a Burger King, someone who I could scarcely understand. But I kept walking along with him anyhow, not knowing what else to do at that point, not wanting to rudely interrupt his emphatic and enthusiastic gesturing with a sudden disappearing act. Besides, I figured I should be open to all available options. Even if I'd had the money, it was too late to find a vacant hotel room in Paris in August. Staying with someone, anyone, might be safer than sleeping out on the street or in the darkness of a park somewhere.

I managed to pick out a few more sketchy details of his life as an Italian immigrant, as we wandered past the Louvre and then crossed a huge roundabout known as the Place de la Concorde, a few random cars careening around it. On the far side of the roundabout a wide walkway went down a long tunnel of trees interspersed with street lamps, heading towards the famous shopping area known as the Champs Elysees.

We were a little way along the walkway beneath the trees when, in the midst of his flailing arms and mostly incomprehensible speech, he made a gesture that, finally, made it clear to me what it was he wanted in exchange for putting me up for the night: blowjobs.

It hit me all at once. The whole choppy conversation fell neatly into place, I just stopped walking, said "No, thank you," turned around and walked back the other way. He didn't seem too troubled or insulted by my abrupt refusal. He just nodded and shrugged nonchalantly, and then kept walking along himself. Okay...so at least I lucked out and got an easygoing pervert.

Now, to plan B. Plan B was, apparently, to wander aimlessly through Paris alone at one in the morning, looking like a lost and confused teenage vagabond who had once again failed to book a hotel room. No problem, I could hack it. Like a cat with its hair on end, at least my pack made me look bigger.

The key factor, of course, was safety. So where could I roll out my sleeping bag amidst a heaving metropolis in the blackness of night, that I wouldn't likely get robbed or tossed into the River Seine or otherwise find myself sorely disappointed in the morning?

Standing there at the edge of the Place de la Concorde roundabout, the obvious answer came to me: why, the center of the roundabout, of course. With cars whizzing around all night and the street lamps perpetually shining down on me, I would be in clear view from all possible angles. No sensible thief would bother me there (and you know how sensible most thieves are).

They would have to "sneak" away across five lanes of pavement with my hefty backpack over their shoulder, hoping that I wouldn't open my eyes and, sans backpack, come galloping angrily after them.

Now lest you consider me crazy, it should be noted that in the middle of the aforementioned roundabout, existed a large circular walkway. And at the center of this circular sidewalk, was a towering stone pillar. An Egyptian obelisk that commemorated the reign of the pharaoh Ramses II, the usual celebrated phallic symbol that stated authoritatively "Here I Was" (that is, before it was moved to another continent). I must confess that I was wholly ignorant of its historical significance at the time. But this lack of information didn't torment me terribly right then. The relevant thing here was the sidewalk area surrounding the obelisk, which looked perfect (in a cold, hard, blinding and noisy sort of way) for laying out one's sleeping bag and attempting some shut-eye.

Thinking ahead (for a change), I wandered over to one of the nearby trees and relieved myself of several cups of coffee. Then I walked across the five or so lanes, dodging a few cars in the process, to the center of the roundabout. I took off my pack with a huge sigh and set it down on the walkway surrounding the stone pillar. Then I sat down on my pack for a few minutes and leaned back against the obelisk to watch the cars going merrily around the roundabout, and generally scope out the situation. Sure thing. I might not get the best night's sleep, but it seemed as secure a spot as any readily available, given the circumstances. I pulled out my sleeping bag and thin camping mattress, lay them down on the sidewalk against the base of the obelisk, squished my pack between my sleeping spot and the pillar and then crawled in, using my smaller daypack as a pillow. I lay there on my back wide-eyed for a good long while, nerves frayed from an overabundance of caffeine and another experience of strangeness, peering up at the clear night sky and the faintly twinkling stars, contemplating the odd behavior of humans, listening to the cars going around and around and around me. Eventually, I fell into something reminiscent of unconsciousness.

After a fitful night's sleep due to the caffeine coursing through my veins, a slightly chilling breeze, the squealing of cars and glaring street lamps overhead, I awoke early in the morning—to see a curious handful of tourists mingling on the sidewalk nearby, with their video cameras focused directly on me. How flattering. I sat up in my sleeping bag and leaned back against the Concorde, rubbing my eyes in groggy puzzlement.

Well, so maybe they weren't actually filming me, but the historical tourist attraction I'd parked myself under. But even that seemed fairly absurd, considering it was a stationary and profoundly unremarkable hunk of granite. Big deal, so it was a seventy-five-foot-tall stone hard-on. Why not just snap a quick picture and move on, leave a poor traveler to his beauty sleep? Although, I must admit it was still a little thrilling, the thought of being on all these tourists' home videos for years to come. Somewhere in Sweden an entire family would be sitting around their living room watching me on their TV, joking about the eccentric, forlorn homeless characters of Paris. My acting debut. Broke American traveler, half awake at the center of a round-about with messy blond hair. I scratched the back of my head and squinted dramatically.

I was planning to stay another couple of days in Paris. (I mean, why let a complete lack of funds drive me from one of the most expensive places in the world?) From there, I would catch a train west and then hop on a ferry over the Channel, full circle back to England. I didn't have any particular plans for my few days in Paris. I'd previously climbed the Eiffel Tower, seen the Louvre, the Museum of Modern Art, Notre Dame, the usual suspects. Really, I just wanted to hang out, walk around, watch people for the day and soak it all up. Paris was warm and sunny now, unlike when I'd first passed through at the end of May. It was late summer and the sun was out, the birds were out, the beautiful women were out, children were frolicking in the parks, old folks were walking their poodles, tourists were enthusiastically videotaping bums on the sidewalk. It was a pleasure just to be there, at the pulsing heart of France and of Europe, waking up smack in the middle of it all to feel its resplendent vitality. Since no one seemed to mind my presence terribly, I decided to eat right where I'd slept, leaning back against the Concorde in my sleeping bag. I had some food in my pack, since I was eating mostly from grocery stores to spare precious cash. I pulled out my camping bowl, spoon, a bag of granola, powdered milk and water bottle for a cheap and easy meal. The tourists were somewhat more reserved about their filming, now that I was fully awake and staring back at them. I ate my cereal contemplatively, watching the endless parade of vehicles buzzing around, occasionally smiling for the cameras. I mean, I didn't want to be rude or anything. Then I packed up, pointlessly ran my fingers through my disheveled mess of hair and hiked cautiously back across the now-busy roundabout.

I wandered up towards the Champs Elysees, through the long tunnel of trees where I'd been walking with the Italian pervert the night before. I decided to get a cup of coffee at a sidewalk café, sit in the sun and watch the tourists and Parisians for a little while.

After coffee I meandered along the River Seine, looking for somewhere to kick back and watch the boats going along the river. I remembered from my previous visit that the Pont Neuf (which means "New Bridge", although it's the oldest bridge in Paris) had a small island beneath it, in the middle of the river, with a pleasant, grassy park right next to the water.

I walked to the Pont Neuf, and went halfway across the bridge where a large open walking area extended from the bridge, for feeding birds, hanging out and watching the river below. In the middle of this open area a handful of birds were perched on a life-sized statue of a man on a horse, once again of some historic significance that didn't terribly concern me. Off to the side, I found a flight of stone steps that went down to the island and the little park.

I set my backpack down in a sunny spot and sat cross-legged in the grass, leaning against my pack. I pulled out a pouch of rolling tobacco to roll up a cigarette, as the river flowed along steadily nearby. Green grass, sunshine and tobacco, the simple things. I was pretty much in budget-traveler's heaven. As I was sitting there with my tobacco out, rolling up a smoke, a thin, attractive, very French woman came up to me and asked, in broken English, if she could roll up a smoke as well. I said "Sure" (as opposed to "Man, you're the one thing that was missing!"), handed her the tobacco and she sat down in the grass opposite me.

While the woman was rolling up her cigarette, some apparent friends of hers came up and sprawled out casually next to her — two friendly street-wise young men, both with long, dark, greasy hair. They also knew a little English and asked where I was from and what I was doing in Paris, the usual questions.

We all sat around in the grass for a little while, smoking and talking, watching the river boats float languidly by, enjoying the sunshine and the relative peace and quiet. Eventually they mentioned that they were going to see a movie — and invited me to join them.

"I would, but I'm flat broke," I said, a little apologetically. A movie sounded fun. But I couldn't afford to be throwing away cash on entertainment at that point.

"Oh, money is not necessary," one of the young men said. "We slip through a back door. We go for free all the time."

"Really? Well, shit, in that case — sure, sounds great. What's the movie?"

"Come with us, we will find out. There is always one around noon."

The movie turned out to be Cry Baby, with Johnny Depp. Like

they'd said, we were able to sneak in through a back entrance, simply by waiting for someone else to exit and then grabbing the door. I didn't feel all too sneaky though, coming in behind them with my big backpack. But fortunately, nobody protested.

It was dark as we snuck in and the movie was just getting started. Lucky for me, it wasn't dubbed in French. Since it was a rock'n'roll musical they couldn't reproduce the singing, so instead it had French subtitles. For free entertainment it was a real blast, especially with my fellow vagabond compatriots.

After the movie we snuck back out into the brilliant summer sunshine. I said goodbye to my Parisian friends and wandered off to find a tourist office. I figured I should probably think ahead and find a room before it got too late, to avoid the opportunistic perverts and gawking tourists in the morning.

But all of the affordable hostels were already full up for the day. The only thing available was a hotel room for forty bucks. Sounds cheap now, but this was twenty years ago, and forty dollars was a major chunk of my swiftly dwindling budget. Fifteen dollars, which I'd paid the last time in Paris, would have been an acceptable splurge. Much more than that and I'd be fasting for my last few days to compensate. I figured instead to chance it and spend another night sleeping out, since it had worked out well enough the night before. And hey, you couldn't beat the price. Then I'd hop a train the next morning back towards London.

After some more aimless wandering that afternoon, I decided to have my simple dinner at the same island park underneath the Pont Neuf where I'd met the Parisians. I found a peaceful spot, cooked up some instant mashed potatoes on my camp stove and hung around throughout the evening, smoking and reading as the sun sank into the obscured horizon.

I'd come across a paperback copy of *Les Miserables* in English my first time through Paris, months earlier. I'd been working on it slowly but surely—at 1,400 pages, it was a monster read. But it was an extremely engaging story, especially having seen in person some of the historical places around Paris so vividly illustrated in the book. I ended up finishing it that night in Paris—not to give away the ending, but one of the key final scenes involves a suicide in the Seine. Sitting there in the grass watching that very river flow silently by, the story came eerily alive.

I considered sleeping right there in the park. But as nightfall neared, I concluded that it wasn't safe enough even by my low, hobo standards, hidden from view as it was below a bridge without any street lamps. Better to be somewhere more visible. Or so I thought. Although the soft grass beckoned, I figured the concrete platform adjacent to the bridge above the park was a somewhat more secure place to lay my head.

I decided to sleep right next to the statue of the guy on the horse, some French king I think. Maybe his bellowing aura of authority would ward off any prowlers. I set up my makeshift bed next to the short metal fence that surrounded the statue, presumably to keep kids from clambering up on the horse. Then I buckled the belt of my backpack around one of the bars of the enclosure as a safety measure, so that hopefully it wouldn't disappear in the middle of the night. Although the spot wasn't quite as high visibility as the busy roundabout the night before, at least there was less traffic to listen to. I crawled into my sleeping bag, and eventually was slumbering away.

I awoke the next morning to the sun shining down on me, just rising over the crooked line of old stone buildings on the other side of the Seine. I sat up, stretched my arms high for a few moments, scratched my head and rubbed my eyes. Then, I happened to glance over at the head of my little sleeping arrangement, where I'd buckled my backpack—to see nothing, where it seemed like there was supposed to be something. My mind was scrambled with confusion for a few moments; until I realized, with a shock that my backpack had apparently walked off in the middle of the night. In other words, I'd been robbed.

I spent a few minutes looking all around the area, thinking perhaps, hoping at least, that a dog had gotten a hold of it and dragged it off somewhere, or some other unlikely scenario. But finally I had to face reality, someone had taken off with almost everything I currently owned, as I lay there sleeping soundly and innocently amidst a sprawling city in a foreign land.

I was, for the next few days at least, devastated. My backpack, in addition to being profoundly useful, had been a symbol of my youthful independence. It represented my freedom, my capacity to simply take off whenever I felt like it and go wherever my heart, gut or thumb tugged me. Also, it had contained a number of irreplaceable items that would have been of no use to anybody else, such as souvenirs and a few rolls of film I hadn't yet developed. I just sat there on my sleeping bag in the morning sunlight for a long while, in a certain degree of disbelief, not knowing quite what to do with myself. In my naiveté, I couldn't understand how this could have happened—despite the obvious risks of sleeping out on the streets of a major tourist city.

But in another respect, I was really quite lucky. For one, I was unharmed. I hadn't, like the guy at the end of *Les Miserables*, ended up at the bottom of the Seine. Stuff was just stuff. In the bigger picture it was of little real importance. A few months from now it wouldn't matter at all (except for that film that I never got to see, damn it). I would, soon enough, get over it. At least this hadn't happened earlier my trip, which would have thrown a massive wrench into my travel plans. And thanks to the fact that I'd used my daypack as a pillow, I still had the essential items it contained—my passport, plane ticket, Eurail train pass, remaining traveler's checks and camera. I also still had my sleeping bag and mattress, so that at least I'd stay warm at night during my final few days of traveling, one way or another.

I called my dad to tell my family the news. They were pretty shaken as well, of course, not only by what had happened, but also by the scenario in which the incident had taken place. Their relief at my being alright overshadowed my obvious lack of judgment regarding sleeping locations. And at least we didn't have to deal with the enormous hassle of obtaining a new passport, plane ticket, replacing traveler's checks and wiring me money. I still had enough cash to squeak by, though the loss of all the food in my pack was another setback. But I told them I'd figure everything out and see them back in California soon.

That afternoon I caught a train out of Paris, utilizing my train pass. I spent the night at a hostel in Belgium. The next day I caught the ferry across the Channel to England, and hitchhiked back to London. Although I was too broke to see anything that required an entry fee, I was still able to see plenty of the sights I'd missed previously, just walking around the city. Finally, I hopped on the plane, that great elevator in the sky, to fly back home. At customs in San Francisco, the United States official asked me why I was coming back from a trip to Europe for four months with so little baggage. When I told him my story, he just shook his head and waved me through.

Part 2

Alaska, 1991-1992

Chapter 6

Hitchhiking may be hazardous to your sanity
(May 1991)

My buddy Josh and I stood on the side of the road outside of Valdez, Alaska, waiting for a ride. We could see our breath as we stood there in zipped jackets, our hands in our pockets. Although it was deep into spring, it was a typical Alaskan spring—cold, overcast, damp. The birds were not yet chirping in ecstatic delight to welcome the new season. They must have been huddled in their nests, same as all the people.

We were about ten miles out of town and the silence was deafening. Pure wilderness rolled away from the road and for hundreds of miles east and west. Cars were scarce—we'd seen less than a dozen in two hours. And they weren't compassionate faces that stared out from behind the windshields. It seemed the people around here didn't have much time or care for hitch-hikers. Our plight wasn't their concern. It was Alaska. If they knew you, or simply knew of you, I'm sure they'd go well out of their way to save your hide. But otherwise, you might as well be a moose.

Okay, so perhaps we weren't yet in a plight. It was May, not the dead of winter. But it could become desperate soon enough, if we didn't get a ride the heck out of there. We might die of boredom and impatience, or even worse: Delusional Hitchhiker's Syndrome. It's not pretty, believe me. Frustration and annoyance turn rapidly to delirium as warm vehicles continue to speed by, the occupants staring out at you as if you're an escapee from the local psychiatric ward. After a while you start to play the part, acting in strange, impulsive, socially deviant ways, yelling and singing into the air, hopping around in circles to entertain yourself, telling dumb jokes aloud to the wind and any animals that might be listening. And of course, the more advanced the condition gets, the less chance you have of actually getting a ride.

But my friend Josh and I weren't the transient outcasts we may have appeared, despite our forlorn predicament. We were just a couple of college kids out exploring the world, on a spontaneous hitchhiking road trip after finishing up the school year at the University of Alaska, Fairbanks (which I had, obviously, been accepted to as it turned out, and my dad came through to help make it happen).

The few paved highways of interior Alaska make a huge loop that covers about a quarter of the state. We wanted to explore as much paved ground as we could in the week we both had free, since this was our first chance to see something of the state well beyond the limits of the college campus and the local town.

So far, we had been east from Fairbanks almost to the Canadian border, then south down to Valdez on Prince William Sound. Now we were headed back north and then west across the Chugach Range towards Anchorage, continuing north from there up to Denali National Park, and then full circle back to Fairbanks at the center of the state.

We'd spent the previous night at a campground on the outskirts of Valdez. That morning we got a short ride about ten miles out of town from a local going home—to smack in the middle of nowhere. We were both wishing we'd stayed near town and waited for a better ride, so we could get a hot cup of coffee about now and break up the monotony.

Finally, we saw another car in the distance coming towards us down the long, straight stretch of highway. We each pulled a hand from our pockets, thumbs extended, ready for action. As the vehicle approached, we could see that it was a large Suburban wagon. Our expectations rose as it neared.

"Gabe, man, this is our ride, I can feel it," Josh said to me.

We held our outstretched arms high. As the vehicle came closer, we could see that the two occupants were both young women, gloriously beautiful women too, or at least so our chilled brains imagined. They seemed to slow as they approached. We both had sudden visions of rescue, warmth and romance swirling in our heads.

It was perfect: They would pull over with radiant smiles on their lovely faces and offer us a ride in their roomy wagon. We'd stretch out in the back seat and have engaging conversation along the way, connecting with the two beauties like old friends, enjoying the pristine Alaskan scenery so much more now that we were moving down the road in comfort. We'd all go out for lunch at a pizza parlor in the next small town, and then continue down the road. That night, the four of us would decide to split a hotel room between us to economize. The next day we would all go backpacking together...And end up falling in love in the wilderness.

It was a classic hitchhiker's dream. But it passed us by. They smiled slightly and waved half-heartedly as they flew past. They hadn't slowed down a bit. It was the Hitchhiker's Syndrome already beginning to set in, a mirage of our distorted imaginations. For a brief moment it had seemed so real, just a few feet away. But then it was all rushing away from us at a mile a minute.

I stood in the middle of the road after they'd passed, my arms raised in protest.

"How could you pass us by?" I yelled after them. "Do you have no respect for destiny?!"

I lay down in the middle of the road on my back and started laughing uncontrollably. It was definitely setting in...

Chapter 7

To travel is to be mystified
(May 1991)

Josh and I did eventually get a ride out of that long stretch of highway just north of Valdez. Not from a couple of gorgeous young women as we had so desired, but instead, from a friendly and robust middle-aged woman, who lived on her own in the Alaskan wilderness. Though who, for some reason, had the heat in her pickup truck cranked up to near sauna level. It was perplexing, in addition to being unpleasant. I couldn't imagine why someone who enjoyed such stifling heat would bother to live in Alaska. Why not just move to Arizona and save on utility bills? (Although, the discomfort on my part may have been due, in part, to the fact that I was all bundled up for the cold we'd been standing around in, which I'd probably gotten acclimatized to it due to all my jumping around and yelling at cars after they'd passed, and laughing hysterically at nothing whatsoever.)

Josh and I would have been relieved at being dropped off and dumped back into the refreshing cold, except for where she dumped us—another forty miles down the road and another forty miles from any vaguely useful outposts of civilization. Except for a large, mysterious power plant of some sort humming solemnly nearby, it was just us, the trees, the highway, and about three cars an hour. It was at the point where every time a car came along, it bordered on a miraculous event. If nothing else, at least we were given proof that other people did, in fact, still exist in the world.

We continued hitching through the rest of that evening, without getting any further. Although it was still a little light out at 11:00 (another month and it would be light 24/7), we decided to call it a long enough day. We cast around to see where we could possibly set up our tents for the night without the likelihood of getting frostbite or eaten by a bear—and discovered, to our surprise, a campground just down the road, that was closed for the season. How convenient, since the only thing the closed gate would keep out was the vehicle that we didn't have.

Although it wasn't exactly perilous arctic temperatures—good thing, since we weren't so prepared—we had gained some significant elevation during our 40-mile ride. There was enough snow on the ground to make it difficult to find a dry spot to set up camp. Eventually, we managed to stake out a dry enough area under some trees and between the snowdrifts. We threw down our packs, pulled out my camping stove and got dinner going, to fill our rumbling bellies, as well as warm our cockles before sleep. (Because there's nothing like a warm cockle. Or was it a warm gun?)

The snow actually turned out to be a blessing, since our water bottles were almost empty and there were no streams nearby. We boiled some snow and cooked up an aromatic dehydrated soup, which we heartily and noisily slurped amidst the chilly silence. Then we set up my small tent on the slightly damp earth, crawled inside and huddled deep in the bowels of our sleeping bags through the chilly night.

The next morning, greeted gratefully by a clear blue sky, we were soon back out on the road. The paltry traffic of the previous evening had increased, barely, to maybe five or six cars an hour. But at least the scenery was gorgeous beyond belief, we were in no particular hurry and despite the snow-patched ground and snow-covered mountains nearby, it wasn't winter and we wouldn't likely freeze to death. Perhaps we would succumb eventually to starvation and/or the terrible Hitchhiker's Syndrome, but we wouldn't perish purely due to the cold.

Finally, around noon, with roughly ten hours of hitching time clocked in at that one spot, we got our ride the hell out of there—

in another pickup, with an old local who took us to the next little town of Glenn Allen, junction for Highway 1 heading west towards Anchorage; and where they had not only an outpost (and probably even an outhouse) but a restaurant. We headed hungrily for the restaurant.

After burgers and fries at the local diner, Josh and I were back on the road. Soon we got another ride, in yet another pickup, with a kind, thirty-something man and his dog. They were going all the way to Wasilla (made famous by the infamous Sarah Palin) on the main highway just north of Anchorage. At that point we would be within a day of Fairbanks, and completion of our weeklong adventure. After our slow progress the past two days, we were ecstatic to finally get some real distance behind us. Josh took the front passenger seat, and I crawled into the camper shell in the back of the truck with the dog.

Along the way we went through some of the most amazing scenery I'd yet seen in Alaska—or have seen anywhere for that matter. Although not quite the same picturesque beauty as, say, Yosemite Valley or Glacier National Park, the sight of this wild, remote area touched me much deeper. The small two-lane highway skirted just north of the Chugach Mountains from across a long, wide valley. We could see the entire mountain range stretched out in full view beside us as we cruised along. The jagged peaks were stark white with snow. And it was evident simply by their silent, rugged presence that this was pure, untamed wilderness we were witnessing, like few places left in the world. The spirits of the natural realms seemed almost to be hovering above the mountain range—a misty haze that obscured them from clear view like a thin veil, hiding a mysterious foreign land.

The sight of such wilderness inspired in me both awe and respect. Part of me yearned to be in the midst of those mountains, hiking through their awesome valleys, rivers and forests, feeling that intense, natural energy flooding my being; that feeling that was the high point of traveling in distant and unfamiliar lands. And yet, another part of me was glad simply to be observing safely from afar, still inspired by the mountains' presence. There's nothing like coming up against the raw power of nature to make you seriously ponder what it means to be alive. I was pondering it already, just sitting there in the back of a speeding pickup, watching through the grubby camper shell window, an affectionate dog draped lazily across my lap.

Chapter 8

The idiot's guide to Denali
(July 1992)

Following my weeklong hitchhiking trip with Josh, I'd spent the rest of that summer working in Denali National Park, just south of Fairbanks in the center of Alaska. After another year of school in Alaska, this time in the state capital of Juneau on the panhandle, I was working in Denali once again—no, not as a heroic and uniformed park ranger, but as a lowly housekeeper in one of the many hotels at the edge of the park. Not particularly glamorous work. But you saved a few bucks throughout the summer, met plenty of fellow outdoors enthusiasts and, most importantly, had the beautiful expanse of the park literally at your doorstep.

I made some new friends soon after arriving in Denali at the beginning of that summer, and we coordinated our weekends so that we had overlapping days off. Every other weekend or so, we would take the bumpy, dusty shuttle bus ride along the gravel road deep into the park together, to explore the untamed backcountry.

There was no shortage of new territory to cover. Denali National Park is one of the largest national parks in the U.S., about the size of the entire state of Massachusetts. Mt. Denali (officially Mt. McKinley, tallest peak in North America) rests assuredly in the middle of the park. At 20,300 feet it towers high above the 2,000 ft. elevation foothills surrounding it, like a mother swan hovering over her baby chicks. When I was going to university in Fairbanks, 150 miles away, I could see the mountain from my dorm room—a little triangle of white jutting above the horizon on occasional clear winter days.

On one of our weekends off later that summer, we (being myself and fellow employees Mathew, Nathan, Hattie and Troy) decided to do a two-night trip that, weather permitting, would give us a clear view of Denali from directly across the wide, flat river valley at its base. Doing so meant taking the shuttle bus as far as it went, eighty miles and seven hours of spine-crunching and dust-inhaling, out the gravel road to Wonder Lake, near the center of the park. But the scenery along the way was well worth enduring the long, sometimes torturous bus ride.

There are few other places in the world where you are likely to view so much wildlife all from a park road—foxes, beaver, wolves, mountain goats, ptarmigan, eagles, caribou, moose, grizzlies and more. And if you're particularly fortunate, with the parting of the persistent clouds you might be treated with the sight of beautiful Denali as well, rising with imposing, craggy whiteness above the horizon. We weren't so blessed to see the mountain on our bus ride in. But we still had a couple days inside the park to luck out.

There was a campground at the end of the bus line beside beautiful Wonder Lake; but we weren't staying there. We had backcountry camping permits, and so were spending the next two nights sleeping in our tents on the open tundra. There are few actual hiking trails in Denali National Park. Since most of it is treeless tundra, one can see for miles in any direction, making trails unnecessary. And even the map ends up little used. Hiking along down the wide river valleys and across treeless ridges, you can generally see right where you're headed and from wherever you've come. Of course, we had our maps and compasses and assorted gadgets of preparedness with us anyway, since you never know when a sudden change of weather or other unforeseen occurrences might transform your pleasant nature hike into an unanticipated ordeal vs. the elements. The previous summer, a young man who worked for the same company we all worked for had actually died after getting lost on a solo weekend trip into the park.

We stumbled off the bus with our loaded backpacks around sunset (being about 10:30, though it wouldn't get fully dark even in the dead of night). All of us were feeling pretty worn out from not only the long bus ride, but also a day of work cleaning rooms preceding it. And we hadn't yet had any substantial dinner, other than some assorted munchies on the bus. We weren't particularly looking forward right then to the several miles of hiking still ahead of us.

There are large designated sections within Denali Park, where one agrees to camp when getting a backcountry permit, to insure that no area of the park is overused. You have to camp inside of whichever section you sign up for back at the ranger station, for each night that you're in the backcountry. We had a park map that made it fairly clear where these different sections were—though sometimes it could be a little tricky figuring out exactly where you were on the map, as well as where the invisible lines were on the terrain around you.

We knew we needed to first hike a couple miles past the campground, along the park road that continued beside Wonder Lake. At the other end of Wonder Lake we would then head up a ridge overlooking the lake (which had a spectacular view of Denali from the other side, if it happened to materialize) and camp somewhere partway up the hill that night.

We had the general plan in place. Now we just had to implement it, despite our collectively weary conditions. Once the bus had lumbered off back down the road and the few other people who had made the long haul headed for the nearby campground, the five of us were left in profound silence. We stretched out our bodily kinks for a few minutes, cinched up our packs and then launched, albeit groaningly, into our hike up the park road.

Sundown in Alaska, as it is anywhere else in the wilderness, is the time of day when mosquitoes emerge in their swarming multitudes, from wherever it is they spend their days. They quickly began to converge on our group of sweaty stragglers as we trekked along, fresh blood ready for the taking. Although we had plenty of mosquito repellent, in these overpowering numbers it did little good.

By the time we reached the far side of Wonder Lake, a mile-and-a-half after being dropped off, we were being mercilessly assaulted by the worst case of mosquitoes we'd ever encountered in the park. And of course, Alaska is about as bad as it gets. There's a good reason why they joke that the mosquito is their State Bird. These suckers were big, and virtually infinite in numbers. Late summer is peak mosquito season and the far end of the lake was fairly shallow, bordering on marshy, making a perfect breeding ground. Word had apparently spread amongst the local mosquito community that victims were sighted, and moving slowly. They soon amassed themselves around us like an inseparable extension of our auras, invading the ears, eyes, nose and under the clothes. Swatting them did little good. For every one that fell, a hundred more brave warriors were ready to take their place and get their bite of the pie. The only thing that vaguely helped was simply to keep on moving.

At the western end of the lake we stopped for a very brief rest, to re-hydrate and confirm our location. After mutual agreement that we were basically where we thought we were, we left the park road behind and started our march through the backcountry, heading up the ridge above Wonder Lake. It felt good to get off the road and step into some real wilderness (despite tundra being a serious workout on the legs, not unlike hiking through sand). Scattered here and there were short, crooked evergreen trees—something called a "drunken forest" that occurs in the lower elevations of the park, caused by the ground shifting when the top layer of soil above the permafrost melts each spring. The trees became like ghostly statues in the pale evening light, watching over the five of us as we tramped along up the hill, each of us surrounded by our own personal cloud of tiny, ruthless vampires.

After another hour or so of hiking we came to a flat ridge partway up the hill. We weren't entirely certain as to which of two adjacent backcountry sections we were in at that point, since according to our map we were right near the boundary line. We also weren't sure if we were a mile from the park road, another rule for backcountry camping. But we did know with great certitude that it was well past midnight, we were all far beyond exhausted, it was only uphill from there. We were at a rare flat spot for setting up our tents; and the mosquitoes were more than willing to transform us into skeletons if given the chance. It all added up to a chorus of nods implying: "Damn good enough—let's camp here."

We wriggled free from our packs amidst collective exultations of liberation from our self-imposed death march, set up three tents in record time, and then climbed in, being sure to leave the tent-flaps open no longer than it took to slip inside. Soon we were all busily swatting away at the mosquitoes that had managed to sneak in along with us. At least we'd munched on those snacks during the bus ride, since we were all way too tired (and no doubt low on blood at that point) to deal with the energy required to muster up a hot dinner.

We squirmed inside our sleeping bags, and with a round of "Goodnight" at one another through the thin tent walls, we lay down our heads with immense relief and gratitude—despite the masses of mosquitoes buzzing angrily a few feet away, and the fact that it was still light out. All that really mattered at that point was that we were horizontal, and enclosed. Soon enough I heard snoring.

About thirty minutes later, those of us who were still semi-conscious heard something, or someone, trudging up the hill through the tundra towards us. I tried my best to ignore the unwelcome sound, hoping perhaps that it was just my imagination, or else a lost moose on its way to the lake, that would surely notice our triangle of tents before trampling us. But soon enough a gruff, human male voice was speaking at us from just a few feet away.

"Howdy, folks. Sorry to disturb you guys—but I need to see your backcountry permit."

"Huh?" somebody grumbled with sleepy annoyance.

"I'm Ranger Carson and I need to check your backcountry permit—you guys are in violation of park camping regulations."

"Shit," I mumbled to myself. And then, "Hey, Mathew!" I hollered. "You got that camping permit?"

"Uh, yeah, hold on…" The sound of shuffling from inside his tent.

"Here," said Mathew. His tent flap unzipped a few inches and his arm stuck out, holding the white piece of paper.

The ranger snatched it and looked over the permit for a minute or two. Then he announced firmly, to our tents and whoever might be listening within them:

"Alright, guys—here's your problem. Number one: you're not in the right camping section. You need to be about two-hundred yards further west, away from the lake. Number two: you need to be at least a mile from the park road, and you're not quite a mile from the road. Number three: your tents can't be visible from the road. Not only could I see your tents from the road, but I could both see you and hear you all too clearly, from the ranger station on the other side of Wonder Lake which, if you recall, you walked noisily past about an hour ago."

"Damn, damn, damn!" I thought…I'm sure we were all thinking. This was absolutely the last thing in the world any of us had the gumption to deal with.

"Oh yeah," he continued. "And how about that bear barrel, you got your food and other smelly items stashed at least a hundred yards away?"

At least we'd gotten that one right, rounding up the food,

toothpaste, soap and deodorant before getting in our tents, locking it in the hard plastic container and hiding it under a crooked tree a ways away.

One of us—I forget who, probably Hattie—then gave him our little sob story, about working that day and getting off the bus so late and the long hike and the relentless mosquitoes. Despite his stern tone, the ranger wasn't entirely uncompassionate towards us given the circumstances. He didn't ask us to move our camp for the night, but simply wrote up a group ticket for a hundred-twenty bucks for camping outside our section, and asked us to make dang sure that we got it right the following night, so he wouldn't have to bother us again. We (those of us who were still awake) agreed—"Sure thing, Ranger Carson"—as he handed the permit and the ticket back to Mathew's waiting hand, and hiked off down the hill. We all quickly drifted towards unconsciousness without further incident.

The next day was overcast and murky gray, though pleasantly warm and dry. It was interesting to see our position now in the full light of day. Sure enough—there was the park road, not so far below. And yep—there was the ranger station off in the distance beside the road, that we'd hiked right past without noticing, while most likely hollering at mosquitoes and loudly slapping ourselves. At the time, the hike up from the road had felt a hell of a lot longer than it now appeared. But as mentioned, tundra ain't easy going. We'd been pretty much on the right track. We'd just needed to keep on hiking a little further up the hill and out of sight from the road, and we would have all been about twenty-five bucks richer, and felt less like inexperienced losers.

After breakfast we packed up and, with assorted grunts of bodily protest, were soon continuing our hike up the ridge. We didn't have too much distance to cover, as we simply needed to make it firmly into the next backcountry section to the south. Good thing, since none of us were feeling terribly lively after the events of the previous day.

It took most of the morning to reach the top of the hill overlooking Wonder Lake. We all stood there with our packs on and admired the unparalleled view for a while; which revealed countless mountains and valleys to the north, stretched for miles back down the park road to the east from where we'd come by bus, and then continued far beyond the end of the road to the west, with almost nothing resembling human habitation before the Bering Sea. If this wasn't true wild country we were smack in the middle of (despite a few invisible lines), then nothing was.

From there, we marched expectantly a little ways south to the other side of the ridge, to see more thick, gray, low-hanging clouds, where Denali otherwise would have been majestically displayed in full view before us. We continued along the ridge in the general direction of the obscured mountain, until we were certain we were well within the appropriate camping section. At a flat spot on the ridge, still within potential view of Denali, we unpacked and pitched our tents. We had the rest of the day just to laze about and work on our manifesting powers, to get the persistent clouds to part and reveal the enigmatic mountain.

But, no mountain that day. It remained overcast all through the warm, gray afternoon and the long evening of perpetual light. Time seemed to stand still for us, with no sun to mark the day and almost no sound other than our own. After dinner we hung around in the extended light for a while, talking and joking. To our immense relief there was a slight breeze and we were away from any standing bodies of water, and thus the worst of the mosquitoes were somewhere far away, no doubt frustrated that we'd escaped their clutches alive.

Eventually we crawled into our tents to crash for the night, still hopeful that we might be treated with a sight of the mountain the following day. Although most of us had seen Denali from other vantage points within the park, this was the closest any of us had been to the elusive mountain—and we knew that we might not get another such opportunity anytime soon.

In the midst of much-needed sleep, I was awakened suddenly by a shout. Perhaps it made some intelligible sense at the time and perhaps not. All I heard was a yelp of exclamation from within my comforting dreams, and I thought, "Great, either another ranger is on our case, or else someone is in the grips of a bear."

I wrestled myself to wakefulness (not too hurriedly despite my consternation) and poked my head out from my tent: to see Hattie, Nathan and Troy standing a little way away on the ridge, gawking excitedly at something.

"What the heck time is it?" I said. The relentless, dull gray light gave no indication.

"About three-thirty, I think. Get up and take a look, man!" one of them yelled at me. "The mountain's out!"

I crawled out of my tent, bleary-eyed and sharing little of their apparent enthusiasm, until I stood up and turned around, and Denali was standing there in brilliant, clear view, directly across the wide valley, the clouds having lifted just enough to reveal it. It seemed impossibly huge. The previous day, the foothills at its base had appeared as substantial mountains, the low clouds hovering just above their peaks. But now they were like midget hills beneath the soaring, white, dramatic peak brilliantly displayed before us, set against the somber backdrop of the pale gray sky.

It was obvious in that moment why it was called the "Great One" or Denali, in Native Alaskan tongue. It overshadowed the miles and miles of eerie, barren, undulating landscape all around it, literally and figuratively. In fact, Denali itself is taller than Mt. Everest. Though the peak of Everest is, of course, the highest point of land in the world in terms of elevation, from base to peak Denali is actually the tallest above-water mountain on Earth, half again as tall as Everest (the island of Hawaii, mostly submerged, is still taller). And here we were gazing at the entire serene, hulking, foreboding mass of it smack in the middle of the resoundingly silent night, in t-shirts and long underwear.

Eventually Mathew also, reluctantly, forsook his slumbering to join us, and we all stood around for a long while in the chill night air, taking pictures in the pale light, marveling at the auspicious appearance of the mountain. Someone, I think Hattie again, had apparently gotten up to water the tundra, so to speak, and was then greeted with the sight of the mountain. Lucky for the rest of us that she had bothered to rouse us all from our tents. This was an experience to savor, both in the moment and long afterwards. It was one thing to get a fleeting glimpse of the peak from the bus somewhere along the park road. Those who got to see that much of it were the lucky ones. And yet, more than just a glimpse, we were able to take it all in for an hour or more. Eventually we realized that if we were going to get any more sleep that night, we'd better get back to it. The next day we would need some energy, as we would be backtracking all the way back down to where the shuttle bus had first dropped us off. But, at least it would be down.

We weren't in too much of a hurry the next day. When we awoke in the morning the clouds had returned, the whimsical mountain was gone and we could feel our weekend coming to its inevitable end. We had a fairly easy hike ahead of us back along the ridge and then down the hill to Wonder Lake, where we would return on another bus back to civilization and the 'real world' (as opposed to the 'surreal world' of witnessing massive, gleaming white mountains in the middle of the night). No big deal. It would be a mellow enough day of hiking, providing no freak storms appeared or other unexpected phenomenon transpired.

We lounged around lazily late into the morning, savoring our last few hours of the silent stillness of the park. Eventually we motivated ourselves to pack up and head out. We figured it would be a leisurely three or four hours of hiking back. The last bus was at five in the evening, so we had plenty of time.

But somehow, things once again managed to go ridiculously awry along the way. Perhaps it was those same unseen forces that had revealed Denali in the night, simply reminding us of their existence, whispering to us not to take our good fortune too casually. It was as if Mother Nature stuck out her invisible foot and tripped us up, just for a good laugh, or perhaps to teach us a little lesson about being mindful of our own footsteps.

We were hiking together along the ridge as a loose group, the five of us in our own introspective little worlds as we picked our way slowly but steadily through the thick carpet of tundra. Once we came to the top of the hill looking down over Wonder Lake, we had to decide which way to go from there—either across the northern edge of the lake, the way we'd initially come, or else along the southern shore of the lake, which seemed a little more direct but would mean missing the easier route along the park road.

We gathered together to confer. Troy was listening to his Walkman and had managed to wander off in another direction, oblivious to the rest of us. We all yelled and waved at him, but he apparently couldn't hear us over his blaring headphones. Finally, Mathew decided to go after him. He threw down his backpack and ran off.

We waited for the two of them to return, for what seemed like too long. We'd all seen Troy disappear up and over a small hill of tundra not far away. It seemed that Mathew should have gotten to him in a couple of minutes, and they'd both be right back. But fifteen minutes later there was no sight of either of them.

At that point, Nathan decided to go off and see what had happened. I had this vision of each of us marching over the hill, one at a time, to figure out what terrible thing had happened to everybody—and discovering either that everyone had fallen off an abrupt cliff, or else they were all sitting in a group on the other side, giggling away.

But just as Nathan was about to disappear over the hill, Mathew suddenly came into view. The two of them hiked back to Hattie and I. Mathew told us that Troy seemed simply to have disappeared somehow into the tundra. Mathew had come over the hill expecting to see Troy hiking along below. But he was nowhere within view, despite the lack of foliage or much else to disappear behind. He had run all over looking and yelling for him, but no sign of Troy.

The four of us talked worriedly for a few minutes over what to do. Finally, we concluded that all we could do was keep on hiking, and hope that Troy was paying enough attention to find his own way back. We could all see the lake just below us, the road along it and the nearby campground, so that you'd be hard pressed to get lost. Hopefully he didn't wander too far in a random direction, grooving to his tunes, before it occurred to him to pay attention to where the heck he was going. The four of us strapped on our backpacks and agreed to head down the hill towards the west end of Wonder Lake, taking the familiar road back to where the shuttle bus would pick us up.

It turned out to be more difficult hiking down the long hill than we'd anticipated. It was a slightly different part of the mountain from where we'd hiked up over the previous two days—more direct, but also steeper. It was choked thick with willows as well as scattered drunken forest, as we dropped down to the lower elevations. We all managed to lose track of one another as we headed down the hill, figuring just to meet up down at the road somewhere. I eventually made it, tired and sweaty but without incident, to the bottom of the hill. The trees stopped abruptly at the edge of a wide-open meadow not far from the lake. I hiked out to the middle of the meadow, removed my pack and sat down gratefully on top of a grassy mound to rest and await the others.

Eventually I saw Hattie come out of the trees a little ways off, and I waved to her. She waved back and yelled that she would meet me at the nearby road. Soon I also saw Mathew coming out of the trees towards me.

"Is Nathan behind you?" I yelled to him.

"Yeah," said Mathew. "He's up the hill a little ways—he's taking his time."

Right at that moment, we heard Nathan start yelling frantically at the top of his lungs. Mathew stopped hiking and turned around, and I stood up. The yelling continued with full intensity. It was a sort of yelling you don't often hear in life. It was primal. He wasn't yelling anything we could vaguely understand—he was just howling away, like he was being eaten alive by rabid vultures, or more likely a bear or two.

"Nathan, what's wrong?!" Mathew and I both yelled up to him. No intelligible response. He just kept yelling away, as we yelled back to him, trying to get a grasp of his predicament. For the next few long minutes we had an exchange of hollering between the four of us that echoed all across the valley. Nathan continued howling away like the end of the world was at hand. Mathew and I continued yelling back to him, that he should calm down and try to speak clearly so we could figure out what was wrong. Hattie was shouting at us from the road, trying to figure out what the hell was going on. And Mathew and I were yelling back to her that we had no idea what was going on. It was like some sort of ridiculous, full throttle shouting contest, inundating the peaceful stillness of the wilderness.

Finally Mathew, once again, decided to go find out what the heck was up. He took off his pack, then ran back across the meadow, into the trees and up the hill. Nathan was still howling away frantically, as Mathew yelled up to him that he was on his way.

Right about then, we heard a mechanical loudspeaker start bellowing at all of us from the nearby road.

"Hello! Hello!" someone or something was blaring at us.

As if things hadn't gotten weird enough already, this threw

me completely off guard. It felt suddenly as if I were inside a department store, about to be told the special bargains of the day.

"Are you guys alright?" a man yelled at us through the loudspeaker (probably, embarrassingly, the same park ranger who had given us the camping ticket). "What seems to be the problem?"

"I don't know!" I yelled back to him, realizing finally where the voice was coming from. "I think maybe our friend is hurt! We might need some help." I wasn't sure whether he'd heard me or not, since I didn't get a response back. And I never found out either, because for some reason we never heard anything more from him. Hattie said the ranger had just driven off shortly after his initial announcement on the bullhorn. He probably recognized us from a few days before, and wanted nothing more to do with such bumbling idiots. Soon after this bizarre twist, I decided to go up the hill and check on things with Mathew and Nathan. The yelling had since quieted down. As I was just entering the trees to go up the hill, I heard Mathew yell down to us.

"No problem, you guys! We're coming down! It'll just be a couple of minutes. Nathan just kind of fell partway down the hill, but he's all right. We'll meet you guys out at the road."

Relieved that he hadn't been attacked by a bear, or lost a leg to crazed bumblebees, I walked back across the meadow to get my pack and hike out to the road. But, there was yet one more riddle for the day—my backpack was suddenly nowhere to be seen. I walked back to the grassy mound where I was certain I had been sitting, but my pack had apparently vanished. I wandered all around the meadow looking for it, but nothing. Finally, baffled, I walked out to the park road where Hattie was sitting on her own backpack.

"Hey Hattie, did you grab my pack, by any chance?" I asked.

"Huh?" she said. "No, of course not."

"Shit, I can't find it."

I wandered back to the meadow to retrace my tracks…and

there was my backpack, resting casually in plain view. I grabbed it and hiked back out to the road to wait for Mathew and Nathan, shaking my head, wondering what in tarnation had just occurred to our otherwise silent, peaceful day.

Nathan was unhurt, physically at least. He said that he'd fallen on his way down the hill, and then had a spontaneous, fed-up freak-out session. No major or even minor injuries, since it was soft tundra everywhere, other than a bruised ego for scaring us all to hell.

Troy also was fine, once we eventually found him back at employee housing later that evening. Apparently he had just kept on walking, digging his music, halfway down to the campground at the end of the lake. He'd stopped to rest, taken off his headphones and then looked around and wondered, "Where'd everyone go?" Then he continued the rest of the way and hopped on the next shuttle bus out of the park, an hour ahead of us as it turned out.

Sometimes mysterious things happen that you never quite make sense of. Life perplexes you with a good dose of the unknown, turning your world upside-down for a moment, as if to whisper over your shoulder, "Don't forget—you don't know what's really going on around here." But this state of not knowing can be as much an opportunity for insight, as for anxiety.

I remember so clearly that brief moment of pure bewilderment—standing in a meadow in the middle of Alaska wondering how my pack could have seemingly disappeared, why the park ranger had inexplicably left the scene after shouting out to us, how Troy had managed to vanish into the backcountry in the first place; and then looking around at the towering mountains, the serenity of Wonder Lake and the green expanse of rolling tundra, up at the partly cloudy sky, and thinking to myself: "Wow, what an incredibly gorgeous place..."

It was a month or so later, as I was packing up and preparing to leave Denali Park and Alaska to move back to northern California, that I heard something about a young man found dead near the north edge of the park. A few months later, back in California, I came across an article in Outside Magazine—about Chris McCandless and how he'd starved to death throughout the summer that I was in Denali, just thirty miles away from where I was living and working.

His story touched me pretty deep, especially after reading the book *Into the Wild* a few years later, which better explained his fascinating tale of rejecting society and hitting the road, and the harrowing circumstances that led up to his puzzling disappearance and tragic demise. It turned out that, at the same time he was hitchhiking up the Alcan Highway through Canada to Alaska, I was just getting ready to unwittingly follow on his heels. I'd taken the ferry from where I was attending school in Juneau that year, through the countless islands of the panhandle to Haines, and then hitched part of the same highway he had hitchhiked through Canada's Yukon Territory to interior Alaska, on my way to work that summer in Denali Park.

Although I can't at all condone his behavior, how he left his parents hanging, not knowing his whereabouts for almost two years as he hitchhiked around the country—hoping to find himself I presume or perhaps just running away—I could still somewhat relate to the nature of his quest. He was it seemed, like myself, on a search for something real, something wild and pure, both within and without.

And he had found it, no doubt about that. Unfortunately, he had starved to death as a result of both his recklessness (he seemed clearly unprepared), as well as unforeseen circumstances beyond his control (such as the frozen river he'd unknowingly crossed, now flowing when he tried to return months later). But in the process it was apparent, by his account, that he had touched something raw and real, perhaps even illuminating within himself. In the remaining few weeks before his lonely death in the wilderness, he had expressed in his journal deep feelings of bliss and contentment. Perhaps he had just gone nuts. Or maybe he'd somehow managed to find that unconditional peace and acceptance that many of us seek, but which can be so hard to grasp in our complex modern world.

Sometimes, finding oneself means going well beyond the comfort zone, deep into unknown territory. It can be hard to distinguish the rational boundary lines at that point. Chris McCandless clearly went beyond that line. But I feel that his intentions, at least, deserve some merit—if not his common sense. As one who can imagine to some degree where his head was at, I think that what he was trying to do was simply acknowledge, and somehow face, the unknown darkness within and see what it contained. Rather than hide from that which we fear and pretend it's not there, jump headlong into it. Get a feel for what exists out beyond the familiar paved roads, in that unsettling foreign land where the moose, grizzly and eagle roam free.

There's another very real and deeply meaningful world out beyond the realm of human perception, which we can glimpse and perhaps even get acquainted with, if we so desire. For the unknown, is truly unknown, only as long as we choose to ignore it. There's really only one way to get to know anything—and that's to experience it. Ultimately life is an adventure, whether we like it or not. Better for the soul to accept this, it seems, and then live accordingly.

Part 3

Western U.S., 1996

Chapter 9

Always double-check the directions (June 1996)

It was the beginning of another adventurous summer and I was at a Rainbow Gathering in northern California, debating which of many possible places to journey onwards from there. As usual there was a plethora of festivals, gatherings, musical happenings and other summertime events taking place in various places around the country. One could easily spend half the year simply hopping from one such event to another—and many did.

But as for myself, I was now on a search for a spiritually focused intentional community (a.k.a. commune) to call home for a while, having spent much of the previous two years living rather sporadically on and off the road. Though I loved the traveling lifestyle, my drifting soul needed something of an anchor for a change.

After moving back to California briefly following my first two years of college in Alaska, I'd settled down for a year-and-a-half in Eugene, Oregon (where my friend Mathew from the bumbling backpacking adventure lived). I'd intended to continue my pursuit of a B.A. in creative writing there, after taking a year to establish Oregon residency. But instead I found myself unexpectedly uprooted, by a series of strange and unsettling occurrences, and by voices murmuring from within my soul, that wouldn't shut up. In the course of a few chaotic months I'd impulsively sold my old Datsun pickup truck, quit my job, stored my few belongings and then hit the road, thumb leading the way. The next two years were spent meandering around the western U.S. on a spiritual quest of sorts, and I was still in the midst of that journey.

I had a couple of different communes in mind to visit; one near Sedona, Arizona and another one up in northern Washington State. I'd been in correspondence through the mail with each of the communities throughout the previous spring. They'd both said I was welcome to stop by and visit whenever I passed through their respective areas. I was particularly intrigued with the folks in Sedona, who seemed to share some similar alternative spiritual beliefs as myself, as well as communal-living ideals. I was also curious to explore the surrounding area, having heard a lot from fellow travelers about Sedona's mystical red rock canyons and the supposed spiritual "energy vortexes". It sounded like a good place for both inner and outer explorations.

The sun was setting behind the dry California hills as I sat in a grassy meadow with some new-found friends, digesting a simple but satisfying meal while we discussed where to go next after the Rainbow Gathering. The weeklong festival in the woods was winding down in a couple more days and we all had unknown horizons. We each had a handful of potential destinations in mind for summer, but no concrete plans—it depended, to a certain extent, on which way the proverbial wind might blow. That was pretty much how I'd ended up there in the first place. A friend had told me about this gathering just a few days before it started, and I'd decided on a whim to hitch there from Oregon and check it out. I thought I might be able to find a ride there from someone headed towards one of the communes I wanted to visit, or else run into some old friends or make some new ones. Anything could happen at one of these events, and usually did. Circumstances out of the ordinary were, when you kept your eyes and mind wide open, fairly, well, ordinary.

In the middle of our casual conversation there in the dry grass, another recent acquaintance of the past few days suddenly came running up to me rather excitedly, from the far side of the meadow where all the cars were parked.

"Hey, bro Gabriel!" he said, panting as he approached our circle. "Guess what? I just overheard these two guys in the parking lot who are headed to that place in Arizona you were telling me about, Sedona. They said they've got room for another person in their van. But they're leaving in, like, twenty minutes, if you want to hop a ride..."

After a brief few moments of inner searching and some urging from my friends to go for it while I had the chance, I concluded: "What the heck, might as well". Having just been discussing the question of where to go from there, I took this as a satisfactory answer—when in doubt, follow the signs.

A half-hour later my tent was dismantled, sleeping bag was stuffed and myself and my hurriedly-packed backpack were in a Ford Econoline van with two Canadian musicians, Natty and Apollo, driving into the fading evening light to make it to a healing and arts fair two days later. They were hoping to make some traveling money there, doing their unique style of sound chakra healing, which involved playing their instruments directed at various parts of a person's body in order to vibrate and awaken their inner energy. It sounded like something that would go over pretty well in Sedona.

Arizona seemed like a long ways to go to make a buck or two. But of course I wasn't about to object. I would be helping them out by chipping in a little for gas, as well as providing some brotherly camaraderie on the road. The traveling pair were in an eccentric free-form band known as *Down to Earth*, the members of which were all from the Slocan Valley in southern British Columbia. They weren't currently on tour, and so the dozen or so members were scattered across the continent for the time being. Natty was a stocky, dark-haired, dreadlocked didgeridoo-player. Apollo was taller, with a cherubic face and short blond hair, and a drummer and flutist.

We ran out of gas twice along the way, due to the van's broken gas gauge. Once along the interstate just inside Arizona, which delayed our trip by half a day. And then, yet again, just a few miles before arriving in Sedona. We coasted the last leg of the journey down the awesome red rock canyons, beneath the orange glow of the setting sun, with just enough momentum to pull into a parking space in front of a church at the edge of town.

Apollo and I piled out of the van to stretch our weary limbs, slightly disoriented by our new surroundings after driving all night and all day. It was evening, but it was still plenty hot since we were now firmly in the desert, in mid-June.

Sedona didn't come across at first glance as quite the intimate, spiritual town I'd envisioned. Perhaps it was the surreal pink tourist jeeps driving around. Or maybe I was still getting used to the relative starkness of the desert. I hoped that things might look a little more inviting after a good night's rest.

Meanwhile Natty, apparently still attached to the driver's seat, had pulled out a flyer for the healing fair to find out where in town it was happening the following day. We were figuring just to sleep right where we'd landed, so to speak, and then get our bearings in the morning.

A few minutes later, however, Natty let out a sharp cry of dismay.

"Ah, shit!" he shouted, pounding the steering wheel with his palm. "Shit, shit, shit! Guess what, you guys? You aren't going to believe this. This thing tomorrow isn't in Sedona. It's in fucking Sonoma, California! We misread the damn flyer, Apollo. We were only a few hours away when we left the Rainbow Gathering yesterday!"

"No way, Natty...let me see that thing," said Apollo, reaching into the van to grab the piece of paper.

Sure enough, they'd just driven all night and all day, to get to the wrong town in the wrong state. But it was a little too late to do anything about it now. And they were too exhausted from twenty-four hours on the road to resist reality for long. After the initial aggravation, they took the news fairly gracefully in their stride, considering. Since I was right where I wanted to be, I found myself torn between happiness at having made it to my destination and guilt that it seemed to have been at their expense (or perhaps due to their abundant marijuana stash), until Natty announced, as a sort of surrendering to the moment,

"Well, hell, I always did want to check out Sedona..."

Spirits soon lifted as they accepted their apparent fate and we all focused instead on where to sleep for the night. For Natty and Apollo it was easy, they just threw out their sleeping bags on the messy back floor of the van. I looked around the church grounds and found a fairly concealed spot just inside the unlocked church gate.

I rolled out my camping mattress and sleeping bag on the concrete landing, and crawled in. I lay there staring up at the myriad twinkling stars in the night sky for a long while, wondering and hoping that I had made the right choice to take that ride. Finally I slept, albeit intermittently due to a cavalcade of thoughts, and the occasional traffic passing by in the warm summer night.

Next morning, while Natty and Apollo were busy finding gas for the Ford Econoline, I called the folks at the community, called Aquarian Concepts. It was a few miles outside of town. They were happy to hear I was in the area. They said they'd like to set up an introductory meeting with me and a few of their members the next morning, to talk about the commune and my potential compatibility there. Then, perhaps later, I could meet with the rest of the community members.

Natty and Apollo were both intent on making the most of their navigational mishap, and had decided to stay in Sedona for a little while to check out the flourishing spiritual scene. If there was any place to make use of their alternative healing skills, this was the place. The three of us spent the day wandering around town a bit. We checked out bookstores and the local health food store, and browsed the bulletin boards for anything interesting going on.

We camped together that night in the woods by a creek near town. We built a small fire to cook some grub, pulled up a few rocks, hung out and bullshitted for a while about our various plans, or lack thereof. Then we crawled into our sleeping bags beside the glowing coals. I lay there for a while pondering once again, listening to the creek gurgling away—which seemed to be having an argument of sorts with the crickets. Eventually they apparently resolved their dispute, and I managed to get some rest.

The next morning, after breakfast, we packed up, then drove across town and out a winding road to a small country house where I was to meet with the members from the commune. Natty and Apollo dropped me off, and we agreed to meet up at the health food store later that afternoon.

The meeting with the Aquarian Concepts community members was—to be as vague as I felt afterwards—strange. After knocking apprehensively at the front door, a tall, slender, gorgeous blond woman with sparkly eyes opened the door, and I was escorted into the living room. There was little in the way of furnishings. It appeared they used this house only for formal meetings, such as the one on which I was about to embark. In the middle of the room were five chairs placed in a semi-circle, seated by what struck me as potential characters out of Star Trek—and one vacant chair opposite, obviously for me. They all had rather intense, penetrating personas and I sat down in my designated seat with a hint of likely noticeable trepidation.

After a formal round of introductions, I discovered they all had names extracted from other dimensions—Santeen, Marayeh, Fane, Jeru and Celestine. I found out later that each member of the community was renamed by their leader, who coincidentally, had changed his name to that of my own, Gabriel of Sedona.

They then proceeded to ask a series of piercing questions apparently designed to reveal the inner workings of my soul, which I did my best to answer (or else dodge). They offered a steady stream of authoritative answers in regards to the world's general state of moral depravity, lack of spiritual enlightenment and all-around modern-day apocalyptic predicament. They continued with a rather lengthy discourse of their version of the true spiritual history of Earth—before, after and including Jesus Christ—with an impressive air of conviction.

They expressed a number of basic spiritual beliefs, many of which I was more or less in agreement with: that Jesus Christ was a revolutionary and a great spiritual teacher; that our current era of history was a time of tremendous change and evolution; that ultimately peace and love is the answer to all the world's many problems; and that changing our inner selves is necessary for making any lasting change in the outer world.

I liked some of the things they had to say. What committed spiritual seeker wouldn't agree with many of these ideals? And yet, for all their lofty, inspiring talk, something about them just seemed out of whack. Although I'm certainly open to and in many cases convinced of some of the more strange and bizarre explanations of the universe, I also try to listen to my bullshit-detector. And it was clanging away insistently at the back of my mind throughout our extended conversation, warning that these folks just might be a ways off the deep end—and not in a good way.

I left the two-hour-long meeting confused and perplexed. They had concluded the exchange by offering me an invitation to come to their weekly Sunday service two days later. Apparently, I'd passed the first test. I felt torn inside with my conflicting perceptions and emotions. It seemed that either these people were eccentric geniuses, beyond my current spiritual grasp—or else they were just your standard cult lunatics on a major self-inflated ego trip. But I honestly couldn't tell. I didn't want to make hasty judgments about them just because they were freaks. I was something of a freak myself, and had always identified to some extent with the cultural rebels and rejects of society.

I hitched back into town to meet Natty and Apollo. We camped again at our spot by the creek. The next day, we drove farther out of town to a different river with a good swimming hole that we'd heard about. It was another clear, hot day and the river hit the spot like an ice-cold lemonade. We spent the afternoon working on our tans, reading and covering some good conversational ground. We built a fire that evening on the sandy beach, and slept there in the sand by the river.

The following day, Natty and Apollo dropped me off once again, this time at a church-like building in town where the entirety of the community held their weekly Sunday service. Dozens of the apparent community members were converging on the building. I was escorted in by the same blond woman, Santeen, who I'd met previously, and I was seated in the front row.

This meeting had a similarly eerie vibe as the previous, on a much grander, more imposing scale. Present inside the church were most of the one hundred or so community members, seated patiently in neat rows, expectantly awaiting the arrival of the community leader and his wife. Eventually, the illustrious couple entered through a side door and took their seats on a raised platform at the head of the room, as the entire audience of devotees stood up, bowed, and chimed in synchronicity:

"Good morning, Prince and Princess!"

I could have easily puked.

A select chorus then started off the service with an uplifting spiritual song, written by the leader—who gave me a brotherly wink from his place on the stage as he recognized me as a newcomer. The rest of the community soon chimed in to the song and, not knowing the words, I contented myself with looking around the room in somewhat puzzled fascination at their intense devotion. I found it somewhat impressive, as well as rather disgusting. They seemed like a group keen on proving something to someone—either to themselves, the rest of the world, God or perhaps, all of the above.

The leader then followed the song with an enthusiastic, lengthy and self-congratulating spiritual discourse. The followers listened with rapt attention to his exhortations against the various wrongs of society—the evil media, crooked governments corrupted by money and power, manipulative religious leaders and the blinded masses who followed them, and artists who gained fame and fortune and influenced society by promoting bigotry, perversity and ultimately their own egos. With equal confidence and enthusiasm, he then praised the righteousness of their own community's actions and spiritual purity in the eyes of God.

He had a colorful and personable style and a charismatic presence that reeked of the message, "I'm a likeable guy, who you can be assured knows what he's doing". He came across as a fiercely moral man—though not one constrained to the usual fundamentalist ideals that make many religious followers seem like such bland robots. His vision was one of a world of overflowing creativity, music, harmony with nature and abundant living—yet all with a humility of spirit and appreciation for the gifts of life.

It was, on the surface at least, a tantalizing vision. And yet there was something about his message and his presence—like the way he'd winked at me—that felt a little too much like a sales pitch, a con man selling a miracle cure to feed both his ego and his wallet. The aroma of the place, its swirling energy of elation bordering on rapture was an enticing one. But as I looked around the room and then spoke with some of the members after the service, I couldn't deny that something about whatever was going on here was just plain creepy. For all the projections of purity and righteousness, what was really behind the curtains of this private little Oz?

I left the meeting in a similar state of confusion as before—and with yet another invitation, to come and see the early stages of their community land and gardens. Although I was becoming more certain that this wasn't the place for me, I still couldn't say for sure if these people were as loony as my gut was telling me they were; or if perhaps I just needed to get more tuned into their higher vibration, and get beyond the weirdness factor. Somehow, I found it hard to accept that an entire group of people could be on a collective course of self-delusion—despite the obvious lessons of history.

That night, back at the campsite by the river with Natty and Apollo, I made a simple, silent prayer before going to sleep—to God or whoever might be listening—to give me a little hand in making sense of this bizarre dilemma before me. I fell asleep with the prayer echoing through my mind and soul.

The following morning on the short drive into town, we picked up a hitchhiker. We were on our way to the health food store again to rustle up a substantial breakfast. We pulled over, slid open the side door of the van and the hitcher climbed in to sit in the back seat beside me. As we continued down the road, it occurred to me on an impulse to ask if he knew anything about the people at Aquarian Concepts, and could perhaps give some much-desired insight into their true inner workings.

"You mean those people out on Red Rock Road?" he said with apparent disgust. "Shit, man, that place is a total cult. They're major control freaks, believe me."

He then proceeded to share a rather twisted tale, involving his mother who had been a member of the community a few years earlier. She had been a devoted follower, along with her boyfriend at the time, when she'd unexpectedly become pregnant. But because the leaders had never really approved of their relationship, along with some other interpersonal differ-ences, it was decided rather abruptly that she was no longer fit to be part of their community. However, they did still approve of her boyfriend. So they'd convinced him to disassociate with her despite the pregnancy, and continue following them. She was then banned from attending their religious services and from the community altogether, and was left to deliver and care for the child alone.

This story sent shivers down my spine—as well as confirmed my gut feelings that something there was seriously out of balance. It also left me with lingering feelings of distrust, disillusionment and sadness, that such unfeeling manipulation could disguise itself as spiritual truth to those not looking beneath the surface. And part of me felt a little foolish for getting involved with them at all, however briefly.

Over the next few days I happened to talk with a few other folks who had been involved with the community. I discovered that some of the leader's many outrageous claims about himself and his cult were: that he considered his group to embody the highest spiritual truth on the planet (hey, that's a new one); himself to be a reincarnation of the apostle Paul (perhaps so—but I'm not washing that one down with Kool-Aid); that he was the doorway to the fourth dimension (come on, everyone knows it was the Beatles); that the energy vortexes around Sedona were of his own making (how old was this guy—4.6 billion years?); and that crop circles were his creations from past life-times (let me guess—and he also built the Sphinx single-handedly?). As my old college physics teacher would have put it, this guy had an ego roughly the size of the observable universe.

I had a brief desire to let the other people at the community know they were being led down the wrong path. But I quickly concluded that it wasn't my business. Was there really a *wrong* path, anyway? If there was any one belief that I wholeheartedly held dear, it was that of individual free will. It wasn't for me to decide another's journey. They were free to learn their own lessons, and I would learn mine. In the meantime, I felt incredibly grateful to still have my freedom, to make my own decisions and choose my own destiny.

Chapter 10

The continuing quest for a good night's sleep
(June 1996)

A week later, Natty, Apollo and I were still hanging out in Sedona, and I was beginning to feel more like I were trapped in the Sedona vortex, than being transformed by it in any beneficial way. The three of us had been there almost two weeks at that point. But aside from my surreal cult experience, perusing the local bookstores, eating plenty of health food and cultivating our tans, we hadn't done much of our originally intended canyon exploring, due to an unexplainable complacency affecting all of us. And having passed on the commune, I now had even less idea of what was happening in my very spontaneous, but rather ungrounded existence than before I'd arrived in this other-worldly desert town.

I decided it was time for me to move on. Do something different. Change the flow. Blow this taco stand. Hit the road, once again and see where it might lead — in which of many directions the shifting winds might blow. My sail (or rather thumb) was set to be unfurled from its mast.

Natty and Apollo planned to stay in town another week or so, to keep some didgeridoo healing appointments they had made with people they'd met around town. Before I took off, they told me about a symbolic Mayan spiritual ceremony of some sort that they were planning to attend a week later, taking place at the Four Corners Monument (at the converging state borders of Utah, Colorado, Arizona and New Mexico). I told them I might meet up with them again there, depending on where my travels took me. And if not, hopefully I would see them elsewhere down the road.

Early the next morning, I stuffed my belongings into my backpack and said goodbye to Natty and Apollo, half-asleep in their sleeping bags. Then I hefted my pack onto my back and hiked down to the highway at the north end of town, intending to hitch in the general direction of the Grand Canyon. Maybe I would hike down into the canyon and have a spiritual revelation of some kind that would give me some understanding as to what the heck I was supposed to be doing with my life. Or at least, I could hope something interesting might happen along the way, which was highly likely.

After an hour of hitching, I got a ride a couple hours north to Flagstaff. Soon I got another ride, about fifteen miles further north on the road headed for the Grand Canyon. After another hour or so of standing in the same spot with my thumb out, I started to get tired from erratic sleep, a constant flow of mesmerizing traffic (mostly tourists it appeared) and the warm summer sun shining down on me at a dirt pull-off in northern Arizona.

I sat down on my pack, resting my hitching arm lazily on one knee, trying my best to stay awake. Eventually, however, I eased down to the ground and slumped against my pack, one arm propped behind my head, the other covering my eyes—thumb still extended in case anyone driving by happened to notice me. At that point, I didn't care about much of anything. I just wanted to curl up in the warm sunshine and float away into a pleasant daydream.

I was just beginning to drift off into that daydream, when a car pulled over along with a large cloud of dust, and narrowly missed me. I quickly came to from my contemplative daze and sat up. I turned my head around and saw that a passenger in the car was waving at me to come on and jump in. I stood up, grabbed my pack, ran through the dusty haze to the shiny sedan and climbed into the back seat.

It was three teenagers from Florida on a summer road trip.

They were headed up to the canyon for the day, before starting their way back east. I was grateful not only for the ride but for their company. Something different, some youthful vigor. They cranked up their stereo with some good, loud grunge music—the Smashing Pumpkins—and we continued north. It didn't take long to reach the national park entrance. Soon enough, we arrived at the huge chasm of the Grand Canyon. We all piled happily out of the small car to soak up the expansive view, and bask in the pleasant evening sunshine and the soothing silence.

After hanging out for a good chunk of the afternoon on the south rim of the canyon, we all camped together at a campground inside the park, and cooked up a big pot of macaroni and cheese over a campfire. After dinner we roasted marshmallows, and talked trivialities with great depth and excitement late into the night. They were a lively and animated group of kids, and gave me some momentum to get out of the funk I'd bogged down in while caught in the Sedona vortex.

The next day, again standing on the rim looking down into the seemingly infinite depths of the canyon, I decided to venture on with them. It was way too damn hot to hike 5,000 feet in elevation down and back up. And it would no doubt be scorching at the bottom.

The kids were going onwards to Telluride, Colorado in the heart of the Rocky Mountains, as they'd heard it was a mellow and picturesque mountain town. I assured them that it was. I'd skied there with my family as a kid a number of times and it was one of my favorite places anywhere. I'd never been there during summer. I figured it would be fun to revisit a bit of my childhood, as well as to get up into the mountains for a change. From there, I'd most likely head back southwest to the Four Corners Monument to meet up with Natty and Apollo for the Mayan ceremony. The carload agreed to let me join them for the ride, despite the crammed quarters. I piled in, and with the music cranking we sped on down the road.

We pulled into Telluride at about midnight after ten hours of solid driving—to find total mayhem. The next day, previously unknown to us, was the first day of the annual Telluride Bluegrass Festival. Hippies and rednecks were swarming the otherwise quiet mountain town, as well as festival organizers with flashlights, reflective gear and walkie-talkies, directing the masses to and fro. They wanted $30 a night per person to camp in a noisy, dirty parking lot—which was not only unappealing, but also beyond all of our budgets. We decided instead to cruise into the center of town and see what was happening. Maybe we would just hang out at a coffee shop or something and stay awake all night.

Due to the traffic it took almost an hour just to get the mile into town and find somewhere to park, by which time we were all fed up with the crowded mess, as well as thoroughly worn out. We parked the car and looked around for somewhere we could possibly crash for a couple of hours.

Eventually we found a landing at the top of some stairs leading up to a local business that looked promising (in an exhausted and desperate sort of way). We hoped at least we wouldn't be bothered there until morning. We went back to the car, grabbed our armfuls of belongings, then tried our best not too look too suspicious as we headed back to the stairway with our loads. We spread out our sleeping paraphernalia, and promptly attempted some collective dreaming.

But thanks to noise throughout the night and a blinding overhead light that never shut off, we all slept—or rather didn't sleep—terribly on the hard concrete. By morning, we were all basically in worse shape than when we'd laid down to sleep five hours earlier.

We decided to get up and look for a good cup of coffee and perhaps some breakfast. Hopefully that would help bring us all back to a manageable state of consciousness. After putting our things back in the car, we wandered down the main street of the quaint ski town in the early light. By now most of the festival-goers had apparently crawled into their sacks, so it had quieted down considerably from the middle-of-the-night madness. Soon enough we found a cozy cafe where we could sit down, relax, slurp a steaming beverage and plan out the day. We were all interested in seeing some live music and joining in the three-day party, while we had the opportunity. It's not every day that you stumble across a hopping bluegrass festival deep in the Rocky Mountains.

But the caffeine, on sleep deprivation, made me feel like I was about to astral project. And the three teenagers decided, instead, that they were going to leave town and continue on their way back homewards. Between the money and the pandemonium, they'd decided it wasn't worth the hassle for the sake of a song or two. I realized that top priority for myself was to get some real sleep as soon as possible.

After we'd finished our coffee and muffins, blinked our crusty eyelids enough times and the sun was up and warming the cool mountain air, we piled back into the car. I rode with them a couple of miles out of town to the end of the valley, where I climbed out and we said our goodbyes. From there, I hiked up the steep mountain range overlooking the scenic little town and the crowds of bluegrass fans just beginning to stir. I set up my tent in a quiet, secluded grove amidst the trees, crawled in and slept not unlike a log for twelve blissful hours.

Being on the verge of broke, as usual, I couldn't afford to actually buy a ticket and get into the festival grounds. But there was plenty going on right in town, including a small stage where bands from the festival occasionally played for free. I stayed there in Telluride throughout the weekend, sleeping in my tent high up the mountain, far from the crowds, and then coming down to town during the day to join in the festivities. I clearly wasn't the only one who had come without a ticket, and managed to have a good time amongst the fellow traveling folk and abundant positive party vibes. It helped a great deal that I didn't have to sleep in the middle of it all.

Come late Monday morning, the festivities were over. I took down my tent, packed up, hiked down the mountain and started hitching back south towards Arizona. The Mayan ceremony at the Four Corners was taking place in a couple of days. Natty and Apollo had said there would be a small, informal gathering convening the day before the actual ceremony, somewhere in the area. I figured that would be a good place to find the two of them, as well as hopefully make up my mind as to what I was doing next in my never-ending journey.

The best way to get to the Four Corners from Colorado was to dip down into New Mexico, and then go through the large Navajo Reservation that spanned the entire area. I made it to Shiprock, New Mexico by that evening, in the heart of the reservation.

After a quick bite to eat at a fast food joint, I was back out on the road, hoping to get a miracle ride close to Four Corners before nightfall. As the sun neared the horizon, and I was beginning to consider hiking into the desert to sleep for the night, a rusty pickup truck pulled over with a Native American couple in the front.

"Hey, man, hop in the back," said the man in the passenger seat, as he rolled down his window a crack.

I threw my backpack into the back of the truck—and found that they already had a couple of riders, a young man and woman also with packs, leaning back against the truck cockpit.

"Hey, you guys!" I said as I climbed in, recognizing them as fellow wandering souls. I was elated to have some like-minded company for the ride—and even more so when I found that they were headed to the same spiritual ceremony at the Four Corners.

It turned out the Native couple giving us the ride belonged to the very family who owned the reservation land around the Four Corners Monument, and they both worked there. They invited the three of us travelers over for dinner, and said we could all stay in a guesthouse on their land out in the desert that night. They also offered us a ride in the morning, since they would be headed to the Four Corners site for work anyway. From there, we could walk about a mile down to where the gathering of ceremony participants was converging. Sweet. Things were definitely coming together.

I relaxed back against my own pack as we continued down the road. I found myself drifting spontaneously into a meditation of sorts. Or perhaps it was just your basic state of wonderment. The warm wind blew my hair back and forth across my face as I sat there, staring fixedly out the back of the truck, the seemingly endless desert racing by at a mile a minute, thinking to myself, "Is life a crazy trip, or what?"

Chapter 11

Love between hitchhikers
(August 1996)

Standing in a scattered field of wild mullein—a thin, furry, chest-tall plant with a yellow-flowered top, generally perceived as a weed—I held my scythe at my side, stared up at the sun beating down through a clear blue sky...and sneezed.

I took off my sunglasses and rubbed my eyes, muttering to myself that this had better be more than just another learning experience. The pollen from the flowering plant was every-where—in my eyes, nose, ears, under the shirt and fingernails, in my socks and underwear. I'd been at this job for ten days with no guarantee of pay, and I was sunburned, tired out and just about fed up.

"Hey, Rob!" I yelled across the field. "Is it near break-time yet?"

"Gettin' there," he yelled back. "Let's go another half-hour or so—then I'll get the truck, and we can load up and head back to camp for lunch."

A long hour later, he finally came rumbling over the hill in the beat-up Dodge flatbed, to collect the scattered piles of chopped mullein that we had gathered together throughout the morning. Bright yellow flower-tops also dotted the field, where we had decapitated the plants before chopping them down at the base. It looked like some sort of apocalyptic weed war zone—and I was the victorious weed warrior, with my trusty scythe. Not that conquering fragile, defenseless plants is much to brag about, I suppose.

Flashing back for a moment, I had indeed come across Natty and Apollo at the Four Corners Monument. The ceremony that took place there was interesting, but nothing too extraordinary. We showed up early in the morning along with a few thousand other curious folks. Some words and prayers were said, people mingled, a volunteer leader of sorts directed everyone into an auspicious formation, some brief meditation transpired and then, an hour or so later, it was over. I'm guessing I wasn't the only one thinking, "You mean I came all the way to the exact middle of nowhere just for that?" But who knows, perhaps some metaphysical tear in the universe was mended as a result of our intentions of peace and healing. Otherwise, it was my first time to the Four Corners, so what the heck.

Following the ceremony, I met up with Natty and Apollo again to see where they were headed next. They'd decided to go to the national Rainbow Gathering festival, which was taking place in Missouri that year. I was certainly tempted to join them. But instead, I decided to go ahead and follow my next lead. I said goodbye, for the last time I figured, and hit the road that same afternoon.

Although I knew the gathering would most likely be a lot of fun, I also knew that at the end of it, I would be once again wondering what the heck I was doing next in my life. And I'd be even farther away from anywhere vaguely familiar to me, and a fair amount of gas money poorer. This summer's adventure wasn't just about having a good time; but I was, in a weird sort of way, trying to look ahead to the future after a number of years of aimless wandering. At the time, the plan was about finding a community to live on that was to some extent "off the grid" from modern civilization—if not altogether literally, then at least figuratively.

So I'd hitched my way over the next week or so to northern Washington State, to try my luck with the other commune—one called Okanogan Farm, near the small Cascade mountain town of Twisp. They also knew that I was coming ahead of time, and had welcomed me with open arms.

This time, the people there were basically normal, grounded folks—even if the usual clashes of personalities took place. But at least their ego trips were readily apparent, rather than hidden from view behind a false presentation of spiritual purity. I'd just as soon hang out with good-hearted, if imperfect country bumpkins than phony spiritualists any day. For the past six weeks I'd been living in a small cabin on their communal farm, helping out in the organic garden or the kitchen, chopping firewood, feeding the goats or whatever else I could do to make myself useful.

Now, the reason why I was swinging a scythe in a mullein field is something of an elaborate story, but basically we were removing the mullein plants from the field for a farmer who considered it a nuisance on his property. Rob had friends in the medicinal herbs business, and while on a trip out of town one day, he'd driven past this untamed field and, upon recognizing the plant; a flickering light bulb had lit up over his head.

To most, this plant was nothing more than an obnoxious and invasive weed. For others, it had beneficial properties. Mullein was an herb commonly used in natural teas and tobacco-free smoking mixtures. Rob had thought it might be a great money-making opportunity, as well as a rewarding experience for us to harvest the stuff and then sell it to his friends. Yet another of his perhaps brilliant, perhaps foolhardy, creative ventures. Only time (and the eventual paycheck) would tell. So far, it had been a hell of a lot of work, and a fine example of an overabundance of testosterone in the workplace.

There were about a dozen of us working together to harvest the mullein, all men who lived on Okanogan Farm. The commune was an eclectic ensemble of two-dozen farmers and gypsy wanderers and their families. At twenty-four, I was the youngest of the adults, admittedly more gypsy than farmer, but intent on working hard when needed (a lot) and open to learning whatever I could from life on the farming community.

Of course, first at hand was busting one's ass in the hot sun while inhaling dusty flower pollen—as well as surviving a work camp with a dozen older men. The past ten days had been an intense mix of both camaraderie and conflict. The latest, hopefully positive development was that Rob had mentioned at breakfast that a friend of his was stopping by camp the next day—and he was bringing along a young female friend, who was interested in herbs and wanted to work along with us to see how the mullein was processed. We all anticipated that this mystery woman would indeed show up, and help to soften the overwhelming masculinity of the past week-and-a-half.

As Rob came slowly down the hill in the old work truck, bumping and squeaking along through the field, he stopped at each of the piles of mullein scattered about and got out to toss them into the back. Wooden planks on the sides of the truck enabled us to pile the mullein stalks up to eight feet high or so. As he finally came down the hill towards me, I stuck out my thumb jokingly, and the truck came to a stop.

"Hey, dude! You want a ride?" Rob yelled out the window at me. "I'm goin' to fuckin' Kansas! Throw your shit in the back and hop on!"

I threw my pile of mullein onto the rest, and then hopped onto the back of the truck-bed, thankful to finally be off my feet for a little while. Soon, we came to the next tired, sweaty worker and the pile in the back got a little higher. After making a large weaving circle of the hilly field, the whole crew lay on top of the huge, dusty load. The truck then groaned its way back to our camp of tents in the shade of nearby trees—our home for the past ten days.

After lunch, and then another long, hot afternoon battling the mullein, we took the load back to camp and spread what we had collected that day out on large, black tarps to dry in the sun. Then we spent another hour pushing the dried stalks from the previous day through a large, noisy chipper, which turned the chest-high plants into inch-long chunks. Even with our facemasks on, the pollen in the air made it almost impossible to breathe. By the time we had finished up for the day we were all besieged, inside and out, with the dusty, itchy, irritating pollen.

Two men got started on dinner, while the rest of us took turns at the solar shower that hung from a tree downhill from the makeshift kitchen. Nothing could have felt better in that moment. It was like shedding a layer of skin. I never quite realized how cumbersome that dirt, sweat, dust and pollen was until I removed it all. Even the dirty clothes I pulled on afterwards seemed delightfully clean, compared to the work clothes I'd been wearing during the day.

After dinner and washing a few dishes, we all hung around the campfire for a while, playing guitar, singing songs and telling manly stories, regaling exaggerated tales of sex, drugs and various feats of idiocy. Pretty soon my exhaustion, and annoyance, took over. I trudged off to my tent to crash and rest up for another sweaty day.

The next morning, Rob's friend Paul did indeed arrive with the young woman, Sandra, as the rest of us were crawling out of our tents and stumbling down to the kitchen area for coffee, and something mushy in a bowl for breakfast. The two had just come from an aboriginal-skills workshop in neighboring Idaho—where people learned to make fire, trap animals and build simple structures from the natural elements, much as the indigenous people did not so long ago. Otherwise known as Y2K Preparation 101. Paul was in his late-thirties, an accomplished outdoorsman and a spitting image of rugged handsomeness—with long, dark hair, clad in handmade leather attire and with a hearty laugh to boot.

Sandra was a few years younger than myself, tall, thin and beautiful with soft eyes, light brown hair and a slight insecurity about her, all of which I was immediately attracted to. We seemed to feel an instant mutual connection with one another, and spent much of that day chopping mullein together, talking and sharing our similar traveling adventures. Suddenly, the drudgery of work in the blistering sun had turned into a great opportunity to get acquainted with a new friend. There was really nowhere else I preferred to be in that moment, other than hanging out in a sunny field with a scythe, talking and sharing stories with a warm-hearted, intelligent, beautiful and mystical young woman.

Through our conversations, we discovered we had some mutual friends from our various adventures on the road. And we also realized we'd practically been leap-frogging one another around the Western states for the past couple of years, attending some of the same festivals and gatherings and even living in the same area at the same time for a while. It was a wonder we hadn't met earlier.

Later that evening, after another long, toiling day of weed-whacking in the sun, we collapsed into a hammock together back at camp like old friends. We knew that we would probably only spend a few days together, before she continued on her way south and I settled back into life on the farm. But still, it felt totally natural and comfortable hanging out with one another as more than mere acquaintances, if only for a short while. Considering our similar lifestyles, we would most likely cross paths again somewhere down the gypsy trail.

To my delighted surprise, Sandra's plans changed. In the course of the next few days, she decided she was curious to come by and check out Okanogan Farm and see what it was all about. She was planning next to attend a logging protest rally down in northern California. But it wasn't happening for over a week. She figured she might as well take the time to investigate life on the communal farm, while she had the chance. I was more than happy to show her around, as well as extend our precious time together a little while longer.

After a few more days of laborious but fun work in the mullein fields, Sandra and I headed back to Okanogan Farm together. The mullein job was wrapping up, and meanwhile they needed a few more hands back on the land. We decided to hitch it, since no one from camp was headed there that day. Weighed down with our loaded backpacks, we hiked across the wide field scattered with countless yellow mullein tops, to the nearby two-lane country road. We hitched south about an hour and then west a little further to the farm near the tiny town of Twisp, nestled in the verdant Methow Valley amidst the remote northern Washington Cascades.

Chapter 12

An adventure in peaceful protest (September 1996)

Perhaps not surprisingly, it was my own plans that changed next. A week after heading to the farm, Sandra and I were back on the road together, hitchhiking in tandem towards the Headwaters Forest logging protest rally in northern California—the same area where Julia Butterfly Hill would soon be dangling in defiant precariousness from a redwood tree for more than a year. Sandra's mom lived in Portland, Oregon, where Sandra had grown up. We hoped to make it there by evening and stay the night, before continuing on our way down to the rally.

We had gotten a lot closer in our short time together on the farm. She'd stayed there during that week, helping out and having fun on the land. Our friendship had blossomed a little more with each passing day, eventually progressing firmly into the realm of romance. After a week of hanging out and having a damn good time in each other's presence, it seemed a silly idea to just go our separate ways to meet who knew when, if ever again. She invited me to join her down to California; and I'd mulled over the idea for a couple of days. Part of me wanted to settle down on my newfound community and commit myself to something meaningful and predictable. Another part of me was ready to journey on and see what was around the next bend.

Finally, I'd decided to make the leap into the unknown and hit the road with Sandra, leaving the option open of coming back to the farm. These kinds of relationships didn't come along that often in my life. I didn't want to pass it up without giving it a chance, just for the sake of shoveling manure and feeding the goats, not to mention enduring the Clash of the Egos. She also mentioned the idea of going to Hawaii to live on the beaches for the winter—perhaps we could continue traveling together if we were still hanging out. I admit that I wasn't against it. My plans were wide open. The farm would still be there. She might not.

After making decent time hitching down through central Washington, Sandra and I found ourselves stuck for a couple of hours outside of Yakima, north of the Columbia River on the Washington-Oregon border. It was late afternoon and we were determined to make it to Portland before nightfall, so we could crash out in a soft bed at her mom's house. After standing in the same spot for much of the afternoon, getting more impatient and anxious as the hours passed, a large, dusty school bus came rumbling down the road. We stuck out our thumbs, with little expectation. But to our surprise it pulled over. Its passengers turned out to be not school children, but instead a band of merry musicians. As Sandra and I were running with our backpacks towards the front of the bus, a smiling, long-haired young man poked his head out the bus door.

"Howdy!" he said. "We're in a band—we'll give you a ride to Portland, if you promise to come see us play tomorrow night!"

"Great! That's where we're headed!" we said, ecstatic for the ride, though quickly forgetting about the promise that went along with it. We climbed aboard, and relaxed back in the spacious bus as we continued, gratefully, down the road.

We arrived in Portland late that night. They dropped us off in the middle of downtown. I hadn't been in a big city all summer, and it felt a long, long ways from the farm. Sandra gave her younger brother a call, to come give us a ride back to her mom and step-dad's house. He was a senior in high school, and eventually arrived in a sleek, black sports car with tinted windows and the radio blasting.

"Hey, sis!" he said, as he got out and gave her a big hug. "What's up? Good to see ya!"

We stuffed our backpacks and tired bodies into the back, then cruised along through the dimmed city streets on the way out to the suburbs.

We spent that night at Sandra's childhood home, where I was introduced to her mom and step-dad, who served up some great lasagna leftovers for dinner. Then Sandra and I stayed up late together, looking at some old family photos of her as a kid and teenager, and goofing around and making out a little. Eventually we crashed out for the night together in the guest bedroom and slept in.

After a late breakfast, Sandra and I said goodbye to her family, got another ride from her brother out to the nearest freeway on-ramp and continued hitching south from Portland down Interstate 5 through Oregon. Sandra wanted to visit a friend of hers who lived on a farm in southern Oregon; and I wanted to stop by my old hometown of Eugene to see a friend of mine, Jeffrey. We agreed to part ways at that point and then meet up again a few days later down at the protest rally.

Sandra and I soon caught a good ride out of Portland, with someone going all the way to Ashland, at the bottom of Oregon, which was in the neighborhood of Sandra's friend. At Eugene, two hours south of Portland, I had him pull over near an off-ramp to drop me off. I gave Sandra a big hug and a kiss goodbye, then grabbed my backpack, strapped it on, waved goodbye and hiked from the freeway into the mellow city of Eugene, which had been my own hometown a few years earlier.

I couldn't find my friend Jeffrey—not a huge surprise, considering he was homeless. I checked some of his usual hangout spots, hoping to run into him somewhere by chance. But no luck. I gave another friend a call, Mathew, but he wasn't around either. I decided then just to leave town and hitch over to the coast, where I could spend a peaceful night on the beach.

I caught a local bus west out of town a short ways to a good hitchhiking spot; then hitched over to the town of Florence on the coast. From there I caught a ride with a semi, carrying a load of ice cream as it turned out, going south down Highway 101. He dropped me off an hour or so later just as the sun was beginning to sink into the ocean. I hiked barefoot from the highway over a large, sandy dune to the beach; and spent that night curled up in my sleeping bag in the sand under the stars.

The next day I continued hitching south down the Oregon coast. I finally made it to Arcata, California later that afternoon—home of Humboldt State University, at the heart of liberal Humboldt County and a short ride from the protest rally. I asked around at the downtown plaza for a ride going that way. Soon enough I found someone, a middle-aged man named Curtis, who was headed straight there himself. He happily offered me a lift. I tossed my pack into the back of his pickup, where his dog was excitedly anticipating adventure in the air. I gave the dog a scratch under the ears and then climbed into the front passenger seat.

We made our way down Highway 101 about thirty miles, then turned east onto winding little Highway 36, and headed inland another ten or fifteen miles. Before us lay the Headwaters Forest, owned by the infamous Charles Hurwitz and his relentlessly greedy Maxaam Corporation. But of course, we couldn't simply drive out and visit this major chunk of pristine wilderness. The thousands of acres of old-growth forest were private property, accessible only by logging roads blocked to public access by locked gates with plenty of menacing signs, to the general effect of "Keep the Fuck Out, or We'll Fell a Tree On Ya". These locked gates were one of the major flashpoints of contention between the loggers and the hippie protesters.

Curtis and I soon pulled into an unofficial camping area for the protest happenings, set up next to a picturesque river in a large gravel clearing, edged by towering redwoods. I thanked him for the ride and wandered off to pitch my tent. I kept an eye out for Sandra. But it was getting dark already, so I figured I'd probably run into her somewhere the next day. I found a spot on the riverbank, set up my tent and cooked up some grub on my camp stove, as I watched the river rushing by and the stars beginning to twinkle reassuringly overhead.

I squirmed out of my sleeping bag to a dewy, sun-spackled morning, surrounded by towering redwoods and Douglas fir, and splashed myself awake with ice-cold water from the river. Then I quickly packed up and hiked back down the highway a mile or so beneath the massive trees, towards the protesters' semi-official actions camp. I'd overheard someone saying that breakfast was being served there, for anyone wanting to participate in the ongoing demonstrations. It was also the best place to get clued in as to what was really going on, since I was a complete novice in the protesting department. Also, I thought that Sandra might have camped there, since she knew some of the people directly involved in the actions.

Actions are whatever protesters do in their attempts to physically stop the loggers from cutting down the trees—such as lockdowns at strategic entrance gates to prevent the logging trucks from going through; staking out manned tree-houses in trees marked for cutting (or woman-ed, as in the case of Julia Butterfly Hill); getting literally in-between the trees and chainsaws in a dangerous game of cat-and-mouse; spiking trees to damage saw blades; and other methods of general obstruction and disorderliness (some tactics of which are supported by various environmental groups and some not, such as risky and potentially harmful tree-spiking).

The actual protest rally, which was taking place the next day, was intended to bring attention to the cause and show support for the more hardcore activists, who would spend weeks and months camped out in the area, doing everything conceivable to try and stop the forests from being destroyed. Although I wasn't such a diehard forest activist myself, I was still passionate about the cause and looked forward to being a part of the experience over the next few days or so.

I was raised in the woods just a few hours south of that area, in Mendocino County, which borders Humboldt County. The trees were a big part of my childhood. My brother and I didn't have TV growing up. Instead, we had virtually unlimited forest at our doorstep to explore, get lost in, romp through and learn from. I wouldn't be the same person if it weren't for spending so much time in the woods. The fact that miles and miles of forest were owned by a company with little apparent concern for either the sanctity of the wilderness, or even the neighboring communities, was disheartening and frustrating beyond belief. To the logging companies, the forests were just a product to be harvested as quickly as they could get away with it. At the very least, I wanted to be able to add another voice to the outcry of protest; as well as show those who had made this their life's work that, as much opposition as they faced, they weren't alone in their struggle against such a mighty corporate force.

Breakfast was indeed served at the actions camp that morning, for protesters who needed refueling. I kept my eyes open for Sandra. Soon enough I noticed her eating nearby at another table. She looked up and saw me, smiled and gave a wave, and I went over to join her. We hugged affectionately, happy to see each other after our separate journeys. I sat down at her table to finish breakfast and talk about our solo travels the past few days.

We spent that day attending a workshop for protesters held at the campground. Some of the veteran activists shared with the newcomers their extensive knowledge and experience—such as how to evade loggers; how to deliberate peacefully with loggers; how to stand ground against angry loggers; and how to call attention to yourself when necessary, or else be calm and quiet and hidden when necessary. The most important thing was to stay safe at all times, and insure that neither protesters nor loggers nor, hopefully, the forest was harmed in the course of us liberal, bleeding-heart tree-huggers speaking our minds and forcefully making a point.

The climactic protest rally took place the following afternoon. It featured a number of well-known speakers and musical groups, such as musician Bonnie Raitt, and drew an estimated fifteen thousand people. It culminated in a march of the gathered masses to one of the property lines for the local lumber company, about a mile away. Police were waiting there at the line to arrest anyone who crossed it for trespassing, since it was known that this was a planned demonstration for the day. More than two thousand people ended up walking across the line and getting ticketed by the police for trespassing, including Bonnie Raitt herself. This was yet another of the many protesting tactics: clogging up the local law enforcement system with too many bodies and mounds of annoying paperwork, and making a strong statement in the process that members of the community were deeply opposed to the clear-cutting of their precious forests, privately owned or not.

Over the following few days, Sandra and I got involved in some of the various actions and projects going on around camp. I engaged in one particularly exciting, though ultimately uneventful deep-woods mission with a group of radical yet fun-loving activists, with names like Paisley, Sky, Dirt, Ladybug, Mudpuddle, Dragonfly, Forest (of course), Wingnut and Sprocket. The small group of us snuck around in the woods a lot, talked heartily amongst ourselves in hushed voices, had a picnic of extremely random snacks, and scared ourselves every once in a while with paranoid imaginings of what various forest sounds might be. But we never actually found the logging operation we were seeking that day. At least we had a good time hanging out in the woods together. Despite the seriousness of the work at hand, there was nothing wrong with having a little fun in the process, especially if it involved communing with the trees.

I suspected that Sandra and I would likely part ways from the happenings at the Headwaters Forest and continue our travels in different directions, particularly if I went back to the farm.

Though we had become romantically involved over the past couple of weeks, and clearly enjoyed one another's company, it was still something of a casual relationship. And though I hoped that somehow our time together might continue, I tried not to be too attached to things. We both had lives permeated with change and uncertainty. Feelings and intentions transformed from day to unique day, quicker than the weather. Probably the greatest challenge of this traveling lifestyle (of many) was that of creating stable relationships.

So I was a little surprised and heartened when, just as I was considering moving on from the protest camp alone, Sandra invited me to join her on another road trip with a friend of hers, O-Live-I, whom I'd met earlier in the week. (His name was given to him by Sandra, who liked giving people nicknames. She'd asked him what his favorite color was, and he said olive. From that, she came up with "O-Live-I"…which sounds like a good answer to the question, "To be or not to be?")

Sandra was considering participating in a massage course that was taking place in the Sierra Nevada mountains in Nevada City, California, starting the following week. After thinking it over, she'd decided to go for it. She was figuring to camp in the woods for the first couple of weeks of the course. Then, once it started getting colder, she would look for another living arrangement. Clearly, she preferred the idea of camping in the woods for a while with some company. And I was more than happy to keep her company, as well as help keep her warm on those chilly mountain nights.

Late in the morning, the three of us squeezed into the front seat of O-Live-I's old Dodge pickup and said goodbye to the protesters and their admirable cause. We drove unhurriedly along the small, backwoods highway that led east through the redwoods away from the Pacific Ocean, across the great central valley of California and then up into the Sierra Nevada Mountains.

Later that evening, we pulled into the quaint, sleepy town of Nevada City. This was actually the same little town where Sandra and I had both been living, unbeknownst to one another, the previous fall. I'd lived there for a couple of months at a yoga community outside of town, while she had been living with a friend literally just down the road. We had no problem finding a good place to camp nearby, since the town was bordered by National Forest land. After dinner over a campfire and a few hours of sporadic conversation, staring into the crackling flames, the three of us spent that night huddled together in our sleeping bags underneath the towering trees and the stars.

Sandra and I enjoyed three more blissful weeks together. We camped in the woods outside of town for the first two weeks. Then we stayed in a small cabin that belonged to a friend of hers who was gone at the time, in the same general area as the yoga community where I'd been living a year earlier.

At that point, I decided I needed to head back up to the farm in Washington. However, I wasn't planning to go back to live there. Upon a fair amount of reflection, I concluded that I'd learned what I went there to learn, and was ready to move on. Besides, Sandra and I had gotten progressively more involved and serious, and were considering future plans once her massage course finished up in another six weeks or so. She had mentioned again the idea of going to Hawaii together and living on the beaches there for the winter.

But I still had a bunch of my belongings back at the farm that I needed to deal with (by a bunch, I mean a few cardboard boxes worth...But that was most of my personal possessions at the time). Besides I was pretty much broke at that point and needed to make some bucks before Hawaii. My dad had mentioned that he could use me for a while working for his construction company on a project that was just getting underway in downtown Berkeley. I could live with him and my step-mom in Petaluma, and commute with him to work each day. In a month or two of toiling away, not paying any rent, I would manage to put away more than enough cash to make our Hawaii plans happen.

Sandra and I spent a somewhat sad and contemplative last few days together, soaking up every last minute of one another's company. It culminated in her giving me an amazing full-body massage by candlelight the evening before I left, showing off everything she'd learned during the previous weeks at the massage school.

The next morning I packed up my trusty backpack, and we walked together out to the main road. We hugged and kissed and then hugged again, and kissed a few more times, and I saw a tear or two in her eyes as I buckled on my loaded backpack, and then turned to walk on down the road. Though part of me was happy to be on my own for a little while, having spent almost every day of the past five weeks together, I knew that I would be missing her soon, and that our reunion in another couple of weeks would be pure joy.

I hitchhiked north through northern California, across the central part of Oregon and into northern Washington State, a five day journey to get back to the farm. I stayed there for a week or so, reconnecting with those folks I'd been closest to in order to say a proper goodbye. Then I'd gotten a ride with one of the community members, who was headed down to southern California to visit family. After several days of driving, taking the scenic route, he dropped me off quite conveniently at my mom's house in Ukiah; where I wanted to stop both to say hello to my mom and step-dad, and also store my few boxes of belongings.

Unfortunately, when I arrived back at my mom's house there was a sad letter there from Sandra, that turned all my plans upside-down. Something strange and totally unexpected had happened. When I'd said goodbye to her, I'd left her at her friend's house where both of us had stayed together for that week. Her friend Tom was an older man, about forty, whom she'd known as part of her circle of friends when she'd been living in the area the previous year. I hadn't met him, since he'd been gone, but of course Sandra had talked about him a little since we were staying in his house and sleeping in his bed and all. He'd sounded like a kind and down-to-earth fellow, who I looked forward to meeting at some point.

But in the past two weeks since we'd parted ways, her friend Tom had returned, and she and him had gotten involved. This was a shock to my system of profound proportions. Sandra and I had said goodbye to each other with the most heartfelt love between us. And, her friend was almost twice our age. It had been only a couple of weeks since we'd seen each other, and her beautiful presence was firmly anchored in my mind, heart and soul. But it was clear in her letter that she had suddenly moved on...and even more so when we spoke to each other once on the phone.

After a few days at my mom's house, trying to make sense of this psychological earthquake in my life, I decided not to change plans after all. What the heck, Hawaii still sounded amazing, even if I wouldn't be going there with the woman who had captivated, and then sadly broken my heart. What better place to go to forget about, or at least contemplate one's romantic sorrows, and start a new phase in life?

I headed down to my dad's house in Petaluma and got started working away as a construction hand on the multimillion-dollar building they were just breaking ground on. My dad knew I was planning to be there just long enough to make some more traveling money. But we were glad to get the chance to spend some real time together, since it had been a while since we'd seen much of each other.

It was a long six weeks of serious grunt work on the project. I was a laborer along with a predominantly Hispanic and very hard-working crew, digging in the dirt, pushing around loaded wheelbarrows, hauling concrete blocks and loads of wood back and forth, hammering, nailing and generally sweating away. But I kept firmly in my mind that vision of swaying palm trees, warm, moist air, radiant sunshine and devouring fresh, sweet mangos and coconuts while digging my toes into the golden sand of a beautiful Hawaiian beach...And soon enough, I was once again striding along through the airport with a loaded backpack on my back, preparing to step into that great elevator in the sky.

Part 4

Hawaii, 1997-1998

Chapter 13

Small world
(January 1997)

I ran into Natty, from the surreal Sedona road trip, on a nude beach on the north shore of the lush tropical island of Kauai, Hawaii. Totally out of the blue. I hadn't heard from or hardly thought of those guys since leaving them at the Four Corners Monument back in June, eight months earlier. Without permanent telephone numbers or addresses it was nearly impossible to keep track of friends made on the road. This was back in the olden days (so to speak) before everyone had cell phones and email and social networking sites and iPads to keep in touch. I'd used the internet just once I think, to find out where a Rainbow Gathering was taking place. I'd pretty much figured I wouldn't see either of those guys again, especially considering they were from Canada.

Backtracking a little...after wrapping up work at my dad's construction site and then celebrating the holidays with family, I'd flown from San Francisco over to Hilo on Hawaii's southerly Big Island, for a two-month adventure. Since I'd vacationed previously on Kauai years earlier when I was seventeen, right after graduating from high school, I decided I wanted to see somewhere new and different this time. It sounded like the Big Island had a lot of exploring to offer.

And it certainly did. But after a week of hitching around the island, I realized it wasn't the best place for a solo young *haole* (pronounced "howlie", meaning non-Hawaiian) to camp out for two months. Before arriving, I'd envisioned other travelers gathered on the beaches, building campfires, playing music and tripping around the island together. But instead I found the vibe there somewhat unwelcoming to blond longhairs such as myself, the hitchhiking slow going and few other budget travelers around at all. It seemed like a better place to come back with a girlfriend sometime, get a hotel, rent a car and see it the more typical way.

I remembered that Kauai had seemed softer and more laid back when I'd been there with my mom and brother eight years earlier. I also recalled at the time hearing a somewhat mystical story, something about hippies living in the rainforest on Kauai's stunning Na Pali Coast. We'd hiked a few miles of a trail which, if you followed it to the end, apparently led to a remote campground with a gorgeous beach, a waterfall, and naked people wandering about, some of whom might have been living there for months. This tantalizing vision of camping out in jungle paradise had lingered in the recesses of my brain ever since.

With this in mind I decided to change course after a week. I spontaneously bought a cheap inter-isle flight leaving the next day from the Big Island over to Kauai, the most northerly of the islands.

Immediately upon stepping out of the airport at Lihue, I felt a dramatic energy shift, both within and without. Even the air seemed more inviting. I could feel right away that this was where I was meant to be exploring and relaxing for the next seven weeks.

I stayed the first night at a hostel in the sleepy coastal town of Kapaa, on the eastern side of Kauai. Though my ultimate destination was the rugged Na Pali Coast, I figured I should probably find someone who had been there before, who could fill me in on what supplies I would need and what to be prepared for (and who could perhaps confirm whether this legend of hippies living in the rainforest was fact or fiction).

The following day was gloriously sunny. While munching on a bowl of granola for breakfast in the hostel's communal kitchen, a fellow traveler suggested I check out Secrets Beach—a nude beach north of Kapaa, a little out of the way but popular with young travelers. By his description it sounded like the ideal place to spend the day, get some sun, swim in the surf, ponder my options and, perhaps, meet up with someone who could tell me about the Na Pali Coast.

After breakfast I packed up, and then, following the somewhat convoluted directions, I hitchhiked to the north shore of the island past the tiny town of Kileaua, where I was dropped off at a gas station. From there I walked a little further down the main highway, turned onto a side road, and took the next left onto a gravel road, which eventually came to a dirt parking area. There was a narrow trail leading from there towards the ocean which I followed, and that eventually plunged steeply downhill through a virtual tunnel in the jungle foliage, to a long, wide, spectacular beach surrounded by dramatic red-dirt cliffs.

The playful waves were a vision of indescribable beauty as I stepped out from the shade of the forest onto the warm, golden sand. I set my pack under a nearby palm tree, stripped down and ran directly into the water. As I lay back in the warm water staring up at the expansive blue sky, the waves lapping gently over me, there was absolutely nowhere else in the world I wanted to be. This was what I came here for. It was the dead of winter, and here I was floating serenely in the middle of the Pacific, nothing between me and the warm rays of sunshine other than my God-given birthday suit.

Later that afternoon, after wearing myself out bodysurfing and otherwise playing in the waves, I took a break in the sand under a palm tree and ate some lunch. A small group of people came down the trail onto the beach, and sprawled themselves out in the sand, not far away. One of them had a big wooden African drum, and began pounding away on it. Enjoying the rhythm, I decided to walk over and sit down nearby to listen and maybe strike up a conversation. As I walked up to the small group, one of the young men with long, dark dreadlocks looked up...and after a moment of astonishment Natty and I recognized one another, eight months later and so far away from the deserts of the Southwest.

Natty had been on the Hawaiian islands for a couple of months. After going back home to Canada with Apollo at the end of that summer, he'd soon realized he wasn't in the mood for another long Canadian winter. He purchased a one-way flight to Hawaii on his credit card, and arrived on Kauai with literally a dollar in his pocket. He'd gotten by the past few months living on the beaches, picking fresh fruit from trees, finding odd jobs to make a few bucks, making friends with locals who would sometimes put him up for a night or two—the usual opportunistic road survival.

Natty introduced me to his group of friends, and we all hung out together for the rest of the afternoon as we swapped stories of our travels since Arizona. As the day wound down and they prepared to leave, Natty mentioned that they were all going to a meditation ceremony the next day, and I was welcome to attend. Perhaps after that we could do a road trip around the island or something—his plans were as wide open as mine. He gave me directions to the ceremony, and they packed up their things and wandered back up the trail.

I spent that night under the palm trees near the beach. I made a campfire in the sand, cooked up some pasta and ate alone to the sound of the crashing waves. I set up my tent under the rustling palms to sleep. Good thing, since a storm rolled in overnight and briefly dumped on me.

The next morning I awoke again to clear skies. I packed up, hiked the steep trail through the jungle up to the highway and started hitchhiking back towards the town of Kapaa. My second ride was, continuing with the synchronicity, a carload of exuberant hippies, on their way to the very same event.

The ceremony turned out to be a purportedly global event. The purpose of the meditation was for people all around the world to gather at precisely the same time and pray for world peace and unity. The belief it was centered around was that our thoughts have the power to affect and transform reality; in whatever way we choose to focus them. The more people focusing their thoughts, the greater the power. And yet, a relatively small number of people can have a great impact on the energy of the planet, through the combined focus of their shared intention. And regardless of the effectiveness (or lack thereof) of the lofty intentions, it sounded like a fun gathering of good-hearted, like-minded people. I remembered that I'd seen a flyer for the event a week earlier at a health food store on the Big Island, but hadn't quite understood what it was about.

A few dozen people showed up for the informal gathering at a lush arboretum several miles inland from Kapaa. We did a group meditation on world peace, sitting in a circle in the grass for about an hour at the designated time, when supposedly tens of thousands of people all around the world were simultaneously meditating. Granted, it was an easy place to feel peaceful, sitting there amongst the lush tropical greenery, listening to the wind blowing through the trees and the gurgle of a small creek nearby, feeling the warm sun tickling one's face and bare chest. Afterwards a few people pulled out various instruments they'd brought, and we just hung out and talked and listened to the music.

Eventually I discovered that a few of the people there had been out the Na Pali Coast, so I peppered them with questions about it. They told me there was indeed a small campground near a beach at the Kalapani Valley, at the end of the trail, which was a tough eleven miles of hiking up and down a rugged series of valleys and ridges. I just needed to bring a tent, sleeping bag, food and the usual camping gear. There was some fresh fruit and other wild edibles to be gathered up in the valley, but not nearly enough to live on unless you were both knowledgeable about the local flora and extremely diligent. Permits were required to camp overnight, up to five nights, which were issued in the city of Lihue. But the valley was little patrolled in winter and lots of people stayed for weeks, months and even years. There were plenty of places in the valley where you could hide yourself, in case the rangers happened to drop in unexpectedly. So basically, I just needed to hit the grocery store, stock up on some grub, and then hit the trail.

An older man named Philip, who seemed to have organized the gathering that day, had brought a bunch of coconuts and a machete. As we were all sitting in the sun talking, he started chopping open the coconuts and passing them around, so we could slurp the coco milk straight from the source. After we'd all drank our fill, he split them into small chunks and then passed around the white meat for people to eat.

As things were winding down, someone brought up the idea of the group of us all getting together again sometime. The full moon was in four or five days. Someone suggested we could do a sweat lodge ceremony for the full moon, out at the Kalapani Valley on the Na Pali Coast. We all quickly agreed this was a hell of a good plan.

Natty and I decided to hike out there together the following day. He was staying that night with his same friends that I'd met at Secrets Beach. I decided to spend the night again back on the beach. We agreed to meet the next morning at the gas station on the highway near Kileaua, and then hitch together to the trailhead at the end of the road on the northwestern corner of the island.

Chapter 14

Sweating it out
(January 1997)

As it turned out, I ended up living for five weeks in the lush rainforest of the Na Pali Coast. I didn't hike in with my friend Natty, however. Somehow we missed meeting up the next morning. Instead I hitched to the trailhead and started the hike on my own; only to meet up with another acquaintance from the meditation ceremony along the way.

It started to rain not long after I headed up the narrow, muddy trail. The scattered showers steadily accelerated into a constant, unrelenting downpour, which persisted for seemingly unending hours. But it was Hawaii, and it was a warm rain. I was hiking along in shorts, with a rain jacket over a tank top and wearing a pair of sturdy sport sandals, and managed to stay warm enough. After trudging along the muddy trail through the endless rainstorm, I stopped to rest at a run-down structure randomly placed alongside the trail, near a small stream that rushed down one of the many green valleys.

I'd completely lost track of time due to the stormy skies. All I knew was that I'd been hiking for many hours, and was getting weary. The ramshackle wooden structure was missing two walls and most of its floorboards—an abandoned ranger shed, I later found out. But it kept out the worst of the rain, and was much better than sitting in the mud by the trail while I took a break. I set my backpack against one of the inside walls and sat down where a few of the remaining floorboards were joined together. While I was munching on some cheese and crackers, someone came hiking up the trail through the deluge, and then walked decisively over to the little shack to join me.

"Hey man, what's up? Gabriel, right? Remember me? Caleb, from the little gathering yesterday."

"Oh, yeah—how's it going?" I said, recognizing him once he pulled off the hood of his rain jacket.

"I'm doing great," he said. "Lovin' this storm, keeps you cool while hiking. I hope it clears up tomorrow though and dries out. Gets old camping in the rain…So are you sleeping here tonight, too? We could make a fire together. I've got a big pot for cooking up something."

"Well, I was hoping to make it all the way out to the Kalapani Valley today," I said, as he threw down his pack and sat down on the floorboard beside me. "You're going to sleep here? I was just having a quick snack and then figuring to keep on hiking."

"This is only about the halfway point. We've come six miles from the trailhead. It's another five out to the Kalapani Valley, and it doesn't get any easier. More up and down, up and down. It's already evening, it'll be dark in another hour. There's only one another place to camp along the way and it's pretty tough to find unless you know where it's at. So I'd say plan to crash here, unless you feel like hiking in the dark *and* the rain."

"No, not really…Dang, I didn't realize it was that late. Ah well, no big hurry of course. I'm just excited to see what it's like out there. Thought it would be pretty spectacular to wake up in the morning to the sight of the valley. But I guess I'll go ahead and curl up here for the night as well, if you don't mind."

"Hey, not at all—love the company."

There was barely enough room for the both of us to lay out our sleeping bags on the few dry planks of wood that were left of the structure's floor. We made a small fire on the ground nearby from some dry timber lying around inside the shack, and cooked up some rice and soup for dinner. We stayed awake for a while, listening to the constant drumming of the rain, staring into the fire and sharing our various wanderings. Eventually we crawled into our warm sleeping bags on the hard wooden planks, as the rain continued pouring down and dripping all around us.

The following day, the rain had given way to clear blue skies. The two of us ate a quick breakfast, stuffed our backpacks and continued on our hike through the vibrant green of the rainforest, still dripping from the night's rainfall. The trail, like Caleb had said, only got tougher as it went up and down a series of jagged ridges and valleys that were the Na Pali coastline. All of these valleys were narrow, steep, crowded thick with jungle and lacking anything resembling a beach, or the smallest flat spot to set up a tent. It would have been one long, difficult and possibly terrifying night of hiking through the darkness if I'd kept going on my own.

But at the very end of the eleven-mile trail, where the rugged cliffs became too steep even for the hiking trail to continue, there was a wide, sandy beach and a campground nestled between the ocean and the steep cliffs. Just past the camping area was a pristine waterfall, which made a perfect natural shower. It fell down a sheer rock face that dropped right onto the beach, the inarguable end of the road for us bipeds. Only a few goats (most of them set free from domesticity by the massive hurricane that hit Kauai in 1992) were brave and agile enough to make it past that point.

Another trail also led inland, away from the beach and the main trail, two miles up into the wide, lush Kalapani Valley. Scattered throughout the valley grew papaya, mango, orange, guava, passion fruit, ginger and a variety of other exotic fruits and vegetables. Apparently there had also been coconut palm trees growing out there at one time. But the rangers had cut them all down to try and keep the likes of us nature-loving, tree-hugging skinny dippers from living in the jungle, since they were a reliable food source. Not that it had worked—as I was soon to find out.

Caleb and I stumbled wearily into the beachside campground

later that afternoon, exhausted from two days of hiking one of the most challenging hiking trails in the U.S. We quickly found ourselves reinvigorated, however, as we came across others from the meditation ceremony already gathering together for our full moon celebration. They had set up camp together at the base of a cliff near the campground, where a large rock overhang provided natural shelter from the rain and wind. There was enough room there for a dozen or so folks to hang out during the day, or else stretch out for the night. And there was a large stone fire pit for cooking meals, complete with a bench made from a broken surfboard and driftwood.

We both gave a hearty "Aloha!" as we strolled up to the camp, and received a round of welcoming 'howdys' and 'alohas' back from the familiar people sitting around the sandy clearing. We quickly unbuckled our heavy backpacks, and with groans of immense relief and gratitude tossed them into the reddish dirt that permeates the ground all throughout that area.

We sprawled out in the dirt against our packs and caught up with the others' adventures getting out to the valley. As we relaxed into the moment and released ourselves from full-throttle hiking mode, we were able to fully take in the remarkable beauty of our surroundings. Swaying palm trees were scattered throughout the surrounding camping area, and we could see and hear the ocean waves crashing not far away. Given our grimy, sweaty state, the sounds of those waves were soon calling us seductively. After a little while of socializing and concerted laziness, we mustered up enough energy to momentarily get up off our asses, grabbed our towels from the bowels of our backpacks, and limped towards the beckoning water.

We immersed ourselves in the waves and lay placidly on our backs as the gentle waves massaged our aching bodies. The view from the ocean, looking back at the coastline, was staggering. Craggy cliffs towered hundreds of feet above the beachside camping area. We could see our group of friends through the palm trees, hanging out at the base of the cliff overhang. Up the coast a little ways from where we'd just hiked, the gently sloping Kalapani Valley itself rose steadily away from the ocean. And the stunningly rugged, burnt red and deep green cliffs of the Na Pali Coast stretched away from us in both directions, with no signs of roads, houses, antennas, beach umbrellas or other necessities of the modern world. It was as if the rest of civilization were an ocean away. And for all we cared at that point, it could have been, and we wouldn't have minded in the slightest.

I hadn't planned on spending over a month camping in the Kalapani Valley. My flight back to San Francisco left in mid-March, leaving me six more weeks on the Hawaiian Islands. I assumed I would probably spend a week or so on the Na Pali Coast, another week or two at other spots on the island of Kauai, and then hop over and explore some of the other Hawaiian islands. But out at Kalapani, one day flowed so effortlessly into the next that it was hard just to pack up and leave, without a heck of a good reason to do so. I figured if I were enjoying myself right where I was, I might as well just stay there. Besides, it was the cheapest paradise I was likely to come across.

Also, I seemed to have lucked out with the weather. Winter was the rainy season on the Hawaiian Islands, and it usually rained a little every day, often for days or weeks without end. But during my first three weeks in the Kalapani Valley, it was clear, sunny and warm almost every day, with hardly a cloud in the sky. And yet, because it was winter and this wasn't such an easy place to get to, there were few other people out there other than our rag-tag group of assorted wandering travelers.

In the course of the next few days more people showed up for the full moon get-together—including my friend Natty, who had been delayed by some personal business. Soon there was a group of about fifteen of us all camped out at the base of the cliff. A few more also set up their tents in some of the official campsites nearby. We cooked up dinner together at the fire pit each night and made music with a few drums, guitars and even a mandolin that someone had hiked in. We spent the days hanging out on the beach in the sun and swimming in the ocean, or else hiking up into the valley to search for fruit or swim in the creek that flowed down through the valley.

As we explored the surrounding area, we all kept our eyes open for a good place to hold our full moon ceremony. Eventually someone found the perfect spot, near where the creek entered the ocean, a little ways off the main hiking path. Amidst a ring of boulders was a flat, grassy area, which seemed almost to have been designed for such sacred ceremonies. There was plenty of room to build the sweat lodge and a fire pit, and still have room for us to gather around. The creek was close enough to bathe in after sweating and the area was clear of trees or branches overhead, so that we could see the whole of the night sky and the full moon, once it came out.

A few of us had built sweat lodges before and knew the basics of how to do it. We'd come across some green bamboo once while hiking up in the valley, which we figured would work well for building the basic structure. On the day of the full moon, we harvested about twenty thin, flexible bamboo branches and took them down to the ceremony site.

It took a handful of us about half a day to construct the sweat lodge. It only needed to be strong enough to hold up a few blankets draped over it, so didn't have to be a work of engineering perfection. The flexible branches were simply impaled into the ground and then bent over to connect with another stick from the opposite side. These were then tied together in the center, about five feet off the ground. A series of eight pairs of bamboo sticks were each bent over in a circle and tied together in such a fashion. More sticks were then bent and tied around the sides to provide further support.

When finished, after just a few hours, it was a small dome about seven or eight feet across, just large enough for a small group to sit huddled inside. The framework was then covered with all of our available blankets, sleeping bags and tarps, to make it as insulated as possible and thus as hot and humid as possible. Like a makeshift sauna, the main purpose of the sweat lodge was simply to get inside, get overheated and sweat. The marked difference between a sauna and a sweat lodge however, is that more than just getting inside and sweating, there is a ceremonial and spiritual aspect to the experience.

While a group of us were busy building the structure, others were collecting armfuls of firewood as well as large lava rocks, which would serve to bring the heat into the lodge. Later that afternoon, we started a roaring fire in a fire pit, five or six feet away from the entrance to the lodge. Thirty or so of the volcanic rocks were then placed into the raging fire and more wood was laid on top of them. We heated the rocks steadily over the next two hours; as people gathered around the flames both to be warmed and mesmerized by it, as well as watch the sun begin its descent into the ocean.

Once the rocks were good and hot, glowing as red as the setting sun, we began moving them one at a time inside the sweat lodge using a sturdy forked stick. They were placed down in a small hole that was dug into the center of the structure, to keep them away from the bare skin of those inside the lodge. After six or seven hot rocks had been brought inside the sweat lodge, all who wished to participate in the first round proceeded to strip naked, get down on their hands and knees and crawl through the small entrance hole into the darkened lodge. A few people stayed outside to watch the fire, attend to the blankets covering the structure and await the next round.

Once all were huddled inside, the blankets were pulled down to cover the entrance, leaving us in stuffy yet blessed darkness. We could feel the heat emanating from the glowing rocks at the center of our little circle of friends. Once everyone was seated cross-legged on the damp grass, facing the hot rocks, a handful of water was poured onto the pile of rocks—and a cloud of hot steam rose upwards to greet our faces and naked bodies. This was when things really started to heat up, and the actual sweating began.

As water was poured, handful-by-handful onto the rocks, the small lodge became hotter and hotter. It took a good while, perhaps twenty or more minutes, for the heated rocks to lose their heat, even when pouring cold water over them. The small space seemed to get smaller and smaller as the steam enveloped us, and some huddled towards the coolness of the ground. The point of the sweat lodge wasn't just to warm up and sweat a little, but to be challenged beyond one's comfort level, and even beyond what a person might think they could endure. Anyone could leave at any time if they felt they needed to. But we all wanted to go deep within ourselves and find the strength to endure and to learn from the challenging environment.

We went around the circle and made prayers, or else gave thanks for whatever we felt grateful for in our lives. A bottle of water was passed around, for those who needed to cool their throats or faces. If it got to the point where it seemed too hot to bear any longer, there was always the option of putting one's face down in the cool grass, and perhaps finding a little air leaking through from the outside. Or else one could simply pray to Great Spirit or whatever higher power a person might recognize, for additional strength to endure the intense heat of the enveloping steam. Sometimes humility and surrendering to the moment at hand can give the necessary endurance to make it through what may seem an unbearable situation. This was one of the important aspects of the sweat lodge ceremony—to be reminded of both our potential inner strength and power, as well as how small we really are in the face of the natural elements.

We all made it through the first round, though not without plenty of moaning and praying. As the rocks eventually began to cool, the last of the water was poured onto them for a final burst of steam on our hot, dripping bodies. At last, we yelled to the people outside that we were done, and someone came to lift the blankets away from the entrance. A flood of cool air blew in on us as the blankets were lifted, and we were all dazzled by the sparkling light of the campfire. We proceeded to crawl out of the lodge one at a time, grateful for the refreshing night air and comforting light of the fire. Stumbling a little with lighthead-edness, we filed down to the nearby creek to dunk our bodies in the cool water, and rinse off the sweat and dirt.

Meanwhile, the lodge was being prepared for the second round, as those who had been attending the fire brought more hot rocks inside. Anyone who hadn't participated in the first round then crawled into the lodge. Then someone yelled down to those of us at the creek that there was still some room left inside. A few went back for another round, while others warmed up beside the fire. This process was repeated throughout the evening as the full moon crested the cliffs to rise above us. Finally the last of the hot, glowing rocks was taken from the dark red coals of the fire and brought into the small enclosure for the last round, hours later.

Chapter 15

Adversity builds character—and hopefully wisdom
(February 1997)

The day following the full moon sweat lodge, most of those who had hiked into Kalapani for the ceremony headed back out the trail—including Natty, who was planning to leave the islands soon. Though we had only gotten to hang out for a few days, we were still grateful for having serendipitously run into one another, so far away from our last experience together in the Southwest. I gave him a big hug goodbye, as we agreed we would probably see each other again someday, somewhere else down the gypsy trail. But of course, we knew not when or where.

A half-dozen other folks stayed behind in the valley along with myself. We continued camping together in the same spot below the cliff overhang, spending the next few sunny days much as we had prior to the ceremony, if a little calmer, quieter and more introspective.

I soon began to run low on food, having been in the valley more than a week. But I really wasn't ready to leave yet. I felt as if I were just settling in to life in this tropical wonderland. But I was going to have to leave at least for a day or two, to bring back some more food and other supplies. I decided to do a brief excursion back to civilization, taking with me just my backpack, sleeping bag and camping mattress, in order to have plenty of room for food. I figured then I would be able to stay in the valley for another couple of weeks.

The next morning, I left my tent standing with my other belongings inside, and headed back down the eleven-mile trail. My plan was to stay no more than a night back in civilization.

The hike was the expected mix of spectacular scenery and views, and intense grunting and groaning up the steep hills littered with slippery rocks and thick, sticky mud. But with a light pack on my back, I easily made it back to the trailhead in a day.

Arriving at the busy parking lot was something of a shock, as it drew crowds of people to the nearby beach. The sudden sight of tourists in brightly colored shirts, clean white sneakers, wearing snorkel masks and fins, screaming kids and people talking on cell phones was a far cry from the peaceful wildness of the valley. I'd fast forwarded back to the modern age. But, it wasn't the first time I had experienced this transition by any means. Along with the annoyances and disturbances of the technological world, there were certainly things to look forward to as well.

I continued hiking up the paved road with my thumb out. Soon enough I caught a ride with some friendly tourists, to the first small town along the coast of Hanalei (and mythic home of Puff the Magic Dragon). By that time it was evening. Having eaten little other than rice and oats in my last few days of dwindling food, I headed straight for the local pizza parlor to gorge myself.

Later that evening, belly stuffed and limbs weary, I cast around for somewhere to sleep for the night. The best health food store on the island was in Kapaa, another forty-five minutes down the road. I planned to hitch there the next day, fill my pack to the brim with supplies and then head straight back out to Kalapani. I wandered around Hanalei a little that evening, looking for a decent sleeping spot. Eventually I came across a darkened elementary school at the edge of town. Since it was Saturday, I figured there wouldn't be anyone there to bother me early the next morning.

I walked into the schoolyard, found a good out-of-the-way spot down one of the covered halls and lay out my mattress and sleeping bag. Clouds were gathering overhead, and I was glad to have found somewhere to sleep out of the rain, since my tent was back in the valley. As usual, my traveling budget was tight. Paying for an expensive hotel room wasn't even a consideration. For a night in a hotel, I could buy two weeks or more of food and then live for free out in the jungle.

But, I must admit, it was a rough night. The thin camping mattress did very little to provide anything resembling comfort on the hard concrete. I slept sporadically despite being warm and dry. My muscles just wouldn't relax, and neither would my mind. I awoke the next morning at the first hint of light, unable to doze any longer. I'd already been sore when I lay down from hiking the previous day. And somehow I seemed even more tender upon waking. Suddenly, the thought of hiking eleven miles back out to the valley with a heavily loaded backpack sounded downright torturous.

But I managed to motivate myself ever so slightly with the thought that all I had to do was tough it out for the next day, or perhaps two. Soon enough, I would be staked out in the valley with a couple weeks worth of food, and nothing else to do other than enjoy the peace and beauty of the valley.

I reluctantly dragged myself out of my sleeping bag and, after rubbing my eyes and stretching out my cramped legs, I got up and stuffed my sleeping bag and pad into the bottom of my empty pack. Then I stumbled back into the quiet town of Hanalei, where I decided to splurge again on a hot breakfast. I would need all the incentive I could muster to make it through the next couple of days. I was feeling much more like taking a long, lazy nap on the beach at that point, than hiking a steep, slippery trail with a loaded pack of groceries.

I hitched the thirty or so miles south down to Kapaa. Kauai is one of the easiest places to hitchhike, partly because you never have far to go, since you can drive most of the way around the island in less than a day. And besides, wherever you end up waiting, it's bound to be gorgeous scenery and easygoing vibes, making wherever you're stuck with your thumb out a good enough place to be for a little while.

I made it into Kapaa later that morning and hiked the rest of the way through town to Papaya's Natural Foods. I spent a good hour diligently shopping, checking down my long list of camping necessities: rice, lentils, dehydrated black beans, granola, oats, powdered milk, crackers, cheese, peanut butter, trail mix, dried fruit, pancake mix, honey, popcorn, oil, herbal tea and spices. Then I went next door to the regular supermarket and got some powdered juice mix, chocolate chips and cookies, a few extra goodies to enhance the wilderness experience.

It was early afternoon when I finally finished my shopping. I now had around a hundred bucks of food stuffed into my backpack. And it definitely felt like it. I knew I had a long haul ahead of me. In my mind, I was visualizing myself sleeping that night in the run-down ranger shack, halfway out the trail to the valley. I held that vision firmly in my mind, as I tackled my first challenge, getting out of town without totally wearing myself out before I even hit the trail.

It was about a mile from the health food store to the north edge of town, where it's easier to start hitching from, rather than in the middle of town. I started hiking down the sidewalk with my thumb out, in case someone might pull over along the way. I was hoping to heck so, since the pack was already weighing me down. There's quite a difference between a backpack stuffed mostly with clothes and other random things, and one full to the brim entirely of food. Imagine carrying three or four full bags of groceries around for most of a day, and you'll get a sense for what I was getting myself into.

Luckily, someone pulled over after about fifteen minutes of walking, sparing my precious energy. After a few more rides, I finally made it to the Kalapani trailhead at the end of the road, late that afternoon. Since it was winter, the sun was already getting low on the horizon. I figured I had another two, maybe three hours of light left. After that I would be traversing the narrow trail by flashlight. I tried not to think too much about the rigorous journey ahead of me. After a quick break to guzzle some water and eat some crackers and peanut butter, I started my slow trek up the muddy, rocky trail, one tired foot after another.

I made it safely along the first two miles of slippery rocks, to the first narrow valley and its small beach. That was where most of the tourists hiked to, before turning back. But I arrived there already completely exhausted. Crossing the shallow creek in my sandals helped to cool my sweaty feet a little and give me some brief refreshment, but it did little to encourage the rest of my weary body and mind.

From there, the trail turned into a massive uphill climb out of the valley. I seriously considered simply sleeping there, just laying out on the ground and hoping it didn't rain. But not only would I have been screwed if it had in fact rained, I then would have been committing myself either to a nine-mile hike the following day, or else splitting up the hike and taking yet another day to get back to camp. My options were all equally undesirable.

I decided to cinch up the pack and keep on hiking, holding onto that vision of sleeping under protection of the ranger shack that night. From Hanakapeii Valley it was another four miles to the shack. But in that moment, considering the setting sun, the extreme weight of my pack, the relentlessly steep ascent ahead and my rapidly debilitating physical condition, that might as well have been twenty miles, or a hundred.

One step at a time, I began hiking up the switchbacks out of the valley. The trail climbed mercilessly up the side of the canyon, ascending to a point of around 2,000 feet above the ocean below. It seemed so pointless, to be hiking this trail up and down, up and down—when both the trailhead and the final destination were at an elevation of precisely zero. And yet, the precipitous mountains and valleys were the only reason why no road had been built there—and thus what made Kalapani such an isolated gem. But of course, this knowledge didn't keep me from cursing those steep, rugged, imposing hills step after agonizing step.

Just after sunset I arrived at the high point at Space Rock (so named for a huge boulder perched at the edge of the cliff, which could be seen for miles in both directions). Though I was disappointed to have missed the sight of the sun setting straight into the ocean, there was some light left and the view was still amazing. To the north I could see Ke'e Beach, near the trailhead where I'd started hiking a few hours earlier. Far, far below me, waves crashed continuously against the barren, rocky cliffs. And eight miles to the south, I could barely make out the ridge that jutted out from Kalapani Beach, my final destination, where, hopefully, I would be arriving intact the next day, if my aching body would just hang in there. After another short break to gulp down some water and munch on a few more crackers, I kept on hiking, chasing the daylight, though I knew it was a lost cause. But I had a flashlight handy once the darkness inevitably enveloped me.

At that point I was well beyond exhaustion, hiking against my body's clear desire to stop and rest for the night. My sore legs and back were broadcasting with amplified intensity an urgent message to my unwavering mind: "Dude, man, c'mon—I'm beat. This is ridiculous. We've got to stop. I can't go on much longer."

But my persistent mind urged impatiently, "I know, I know, it's rough going. I'm feeling it too. But let's just make it a few more miles, and then we'll be at a great spot to sleep comfortably for the night. Trust me, we can do it."

"A few more miles?!" my body exasperated. "Shit man, I'm not sure if I'm going to make it a few more *yards*, let alone miles! Why can't we just sleep right here in the middle of the path? I'm sure no one will come along before morning. Doesn't this look like a pretty good spot? It looks so comfy. There are only a few clouds,

I'm sure it won't rain tonight..."

"Yeah, but if it does, then we'll both be miserable—and then *you'll* be bitching at *me* for not planning things out better. Look, let's just keep going a little longer, and we'll assess the situation further down the trail."

"Well, alright..." my tired body grumbled. After all, when it came down to it, the mind made the decisions.

With that, I forced myself to continue hiking, one small step in front of the other, a few long yards at a time. The sky eventually darkened. I pulled my flashlight out of my pack, stumbling my way through the dark in a daze, as the trail led up and down more valleys, through forests and along ridges suspended high above the water. I did my best to enjoy the beautiful views of the boundless ocean reflecting the starlight, and the rhythmic sounds of the waves crashing far below.

At one point I started singing out loud, both to keep myself awake as well as to scare off any wild boars, goats, rabid cats or other animals that might be prowling in the area. Mostly though, it was just to keep myself going. As my mind and body continued arguing over whether to continue on through the night, or simply collapse at the next vaguely flat spot and fade into blessed unconsciousness, I progressed from singing, to yelling at the top of my lungs—at myself, the trail, the mountains, the ocean, the scattered clouds and even the waning moon appearing on the ocean's horizon. As my body became more and more debilitated with each laborious step, I had to somehow drown out my misery—and yelling seemed to do the trick. I'd gone so far beyond exhaustion by that point that the added effort of yelling no longer made any difference. I was going to be miserable as long as I was stuck in this predicament. And a noisy, incoherent misery was somehow better right then than a silently trudging one.

Next, I turned to shouting out ridiculous, made-up jokes at myself, as well as laughing hysterically as I hiked through the blackness. Something akin to the Delusional Hitchhiker's Syndrome began to set in, in this case, Delirious Backpacker's Disorder. I momentarily lost my grip on reality, not from boredom in this case, but instead from overwhelming bodily fatigue. At least, this time, my loss of sanity wouldn't affect my ability to reach my destination. It would be my own dogged persistence, and not the willing assistance of complete strangers that would get me out of this fix. I could behave as ridiculously as I honestly felt at the time, and there was no one around to care other than, perhaps, a few freaked-out goats and pigs.

Finally, to my virtual disbelief, my relentless persistence paid off. I rounded a bend and recognized a hill on the trail as the final descent into the valley where the ranger shack was located. From there it was another quarter-mile hike to the creek and the dilapidated little structure that would be my budget hotel for the night. I would, it appeared, survive another day.

Upon arriving, I set my pack down inside the shack with both a sigh of relief and a groan that went on for several minutes. Too tired to fix up a real dinner, I simply ate some trail mix and dried fruit, and then laid out my sleeping bag on the hard wooden planks. My body was so tense from its forced march, that it took hours before I was able to relax enough to fall asleep—if you could even call it that.

I awoke too early, once again, due to the hard surface and my sore, worn out muscles pulsing with unrelenting misery. After laying there on the wooden planks for a little while, pondering my anguish, wishing like hell that I didn't have another accursed day of hiking ahead of me, I reluctantly got up, ate some dry granola and packed up. Too soon I was back out on the trail, amidst more perpetual groaning and bodily protest. My pack seemed to be filled with lead weights, and my legs felt like they were made of them.

I continued trudging along, one torturous step at a time, this time envisioning myself sleeping cozily in my tent that night. At least I had the entire day to hike the last five miles, rather than a dimming sliver of an evening. I was certain I could make it as long as I kept my mind set on the prize, another week or two in paradise.

I finally stumbled into camp late that afternoon. My fellow traveling friends were apparently gone for the day, probably out exploring the valley. This didn't bother me in the slightest. I was too exhausted, physically, mentally and emotionally to talk or relate to anyone anyway. I zipped open my tent, lay out my sleeping bag inside and crawled in, dragging my well-earned pack full of food in beside me. I just lay there for a long while, listening to the nearby ocean waves and palm trees rustling overhead, happy to finally be motionless. Eventually I must have fallen asleep, because I no longer hurt.

The next day I decided to move my camp up into the valley, away from the beach and the few tourists who were camped nearby. Just a few folks were left from the sweat lodge ceremony, and I'd decided I wanted a little solo time for a while. I hiked all of my food and belongings about a mile up into the valley, and assembled my camp at a flat spot under a large mango tree, near the creek that ran down through the valley and into the ocean.

Over the following days and weeks of exploring the valley, I happened across a number of things that other people had left behind in the woods: a teapot, rusty beach chair, small mattress, extra blanket and pillow, pots and pans. Pretty soon my little camp began to feel more or less like a true home.

I eased into a daily routine, waking each morning to make tea and oatmeal or pancakes over a fire. I would lounge around in the cool morning air in my long underwear, until the sun came out and warmed things up a bit. Since it was winter, it did get chilly at times, especially whenever a storm blew through. After the first few weeks of sun, the more typical winter Hawaiian weather returned, with frequent showers and even hard-driving rain.

After breakfast I went down to the nearby creek to dunk my head and wash up. Then I hiked up into the valley to look for any ripe fruit, such as papaya, guava or oranges. Unfortunately mango wasn't yet in season, or else I would have had fruit dropping all around my campsite. In the afternoons I hiked down to the beach. Then I would hike back up to my camp by dinnertime.

One day, while down on the beach waiting for the sun to set, a couple of traveling folks that I didn't yet know wandered by and stopped to talk. A young woman with dark dreadlocks, who introduced herself as Aiko, mentioned that they were cooking up a communal dinner by the beach every night—and anyone was welcome to join in, as long as they brought something to contribute. I told them my camp was up in the valley, so I didn't have any food with me right then—but I would probably join them the next night. Having spent much of the past week alone, I was now in the mood for a little company.

The following day I hiked down from the valley with some dry lentils, garlic, onion and spices, and spent the afternoon reading on the beach. As evening approached, I wandered over to the place that Aiko had mentioned, a grassy area right near the beach. As the sun was about to set, Aiko and some other folks showed up and we all started cooking dinner together. They were camped in the trees nearby, and had brought a big pot in which to cook everything. In addition to my food offerings, there were more lentils and garlic, rice, potatoes, carrots, garbanzo beans and more spices.

We got a good fire going, then filled the huge pot partly with seawater, and the rest of the way with fresh water from the waterfall. Once the water was boiling away, the random assortment of food was cut into bite-sized pieces and then tossed into the pot. We named it "Kalapani Stew". Somehow it was always delicious, despite our experimentation and complete lack of discretion; whatever anyone brought went into the pot.

Undoubtedly the sunset, soothing ocean waves, incredible scenery and good company were as important elements as the actual ingredients that went into our dinner.

Over the next few weeks I hiked down to have dinner by the beach almost every evening. I was rarely wearing sandals by now, and often spent the day nude or else in a thin cotton sarong. Over the course of five weeks in the valley my feet toughened up, so that I became comfortable hiking around the jungle trails in my bare feet.

Once, however, I was bitten on the toe by a poisonous centipede. They have these huge, nasty centipedes on the Hawaiian Islands that can get close to a foot long and three-quarters of an inch wide. They look like some sort of strange armored robot toy, and have a fairly poisonous bite. Although they won't kill you, some people have a strong reaction to them and can get pretty ill. But most simply go through some serious pain for twenty or thirty minutes, before it subsides and leaves an itchy bump for a few days. Although they aren't seen regularly, their presence is something of a legend amongst campers, which occasionally brings itself to life.

As I was walking barefoot down the valley trail one night with some friends, headed to one of their camps, I felt suddenly as if my toe had been slammed with a hammer, though I knew I hadn't hit it on a rock. I yelped and leapt into the air. Because it was dark, I couldn't see whatever had gotten me, so I just kept walking along with something of a limp. When we got back to a campfire, we were able to find the spot where the centipede had gotten its little fangs into me. Lucky for me, I didn't have a bad reaction to it, just some pain to endure for a few hours until it calmed down, as the poison worked its way through my system. I took the experience as something of an initiation into the valley, to remind me who really owned the place—the bugs, birds and trees—and who would be there long after I left.

Chapter 16

Close call
(March 1997)

One of my more profound, and perilous experiences in the Kalapani Valley came shortly before planning to leave. Three weeks after my exhausting supply run, it was time to restock again. Fortunately the food had lasted even longer than I'd expected. But I wanted to stay one more week in the valley. So I geared up to do the hike out to civilization and back once again. This time I decided to bring my tent, since I wouldn't have such a ridiculously heavy load of food. I planned to spend the night sleeping at Secrets Beach, to give myself the chance to rejuvenate for the hike back in.

Once again, I hiked the arduous eleven-mile coastal trail in a day thanks to the light load. I arrived at the busy parking lot near the trailhead late in the afternoon, and hitched past Hanalei to the next town of Kileaua, near the trail down to Secrets Beach.

I hiked the steep trail down to the spectacular beach, where I'd spent the night alone a month earlier...to find a virtual village of travelers camped in the palm trees near the sand. Over the past month word had apparently spread that this was a good place to camp. Or perhaps, since spring was approaching, there were simply more travelers coming out to the island. Dozens of rough and ragged wanderers were scattered about, swimming in the ocean, playing frisbee or else sitting around campfires talking and cooking up dinner. I set up my own tent amidst the throng, and joined a group around a campfire to cook my own dinner and catch up on any news I'd missed in the past month of isolation.

The next day I left my tent set up by the beach and hitched

down to Kapaa to do my food shopping again at Papaya's. Then I headed back with my load, to relax at the beach with the rest of the traveling crew for the afternoon.

Later that evening, while sitting with some people around a flickering campfire, I happened to mention that I was hiking out to the Kalapani Valley the next day. A young woman around the fire, Carissa, said she had been planning to go out there as well, and asked if she might join me for the hike. I gladly invited her to come along. The next morning we packed up and hitchhiked together to the trailhead at the end of the road. Due to an early start and relatively light packs, we managed to hike out to the valley in a single day.

After four or five days of hanging out together in Kalapani, Carissa and I decided to do a fast. We were both leaving the valley in a few more days, and then leaving Hawaii altogether to go back home. We thought that a physical and spiritual cleanse would help the transition from this incomparable paradise back to the modern world.

On the second day of fasting, feeling weak and depleted but still in good health, we went for a swim in the ocean to cool ourselves. We figured we would just go in a little ways, since we knew we weren't strong enough to tackle any strong waves. We walked down to the beach and waded into the water. It was both refreshing and invigorating to plunge into the cool ocean. We lay back in the shallow water as the inviting waves splashed steadily over us, and the sun shone down upon our bodies.

Somehow, Carissa managed to drift into deeper water, although she was still fairly close to shore. As I lay there staring up into the sky, I suddenly heard her yelling for help. I stood up in the waist-deep water, and though she wasn't far away from me, it was apparent that she had gotten sucked into a riptide. She was struggling desperately to stay afloat, since the waves had unexpectedly picked up and were now crashing over her head. Instinctively, I swam out to try to grab her and bring her back to shore.

But because of our frail condition, I quickly realized that I could barely keep myself afloat, not to mention the both of us. I had to let her go just to keep myself from drowning. I realized then how weak I truly was from fasting, as the waves crashed over me and I struggled to keep my own head above water. I could touch the sand below only by dunking my head, and then pushing off to get my head back out of the water. And like most people in that situation, I made the mistake of setting my sights on the shore and fighting the waves and current in the process, rather than swimming sideways and seeking shallower water that way. This deep water was the same distance from the beach as where I'd been standing waist-deep just a minute earlier. I should have swum back to where I'd been standing. But in the distress of the life-threatening moment, which is too often how it goes, I just didn't think.

As my strength quickly waned I went into a blind panic, swimming furiously against the waves, draining precious energy in the process. I knew that drowning was now a very real possibility. And I knew also that this wasn't something I was ready to accept. As much as I loved this valley, I didn't want to be there forever. But unless I managed to fight for my life, as well as luck out, then the ocean waves were going to take me down and I wouldn't be coming back up alive.

I fought to stay afloat as much as my scant strength afforded me. And then somehow, things suddenly changed. I must have drifted back over to where I'd been standing before, because all of a sudden the deep water became shallow and I was able to struggle to my feet.

I then turned around, expecting to witness a terrible image of Carissa either floating unconscious in the water or else nowhere to be seen. But incredibly, though she was a long ways behind me, she too had come to shallow water and was now stumbling through the waves towards me. Once we both made it out of the water, we collapsed in the hot, dry sand, silently thanking God for the chance to continue on with our precious lives, and not be more victims of the whimsical Hawaiian waves.

Carissa and I broke our fast soon after that terrifying experience, to get our strength back, physically, mentally and spiritually. And a few days later, we hiked out of the valley together. We both planned to camp down at Secrets Beach for a little while and enjoy the company of like-minded souls. Also my friend Aiko and I had agreed to meet up there in a couple of days, since she was hopping over to Maui the same day that I was flying back to the mainland.

I spent my last few days camping amidst the ramshackle traveler's village at Secrets Beach; and during the day did a bit more exploring around the rest of the island with other travelers. Aiko showed up the evening before we both were flying out, and camped on the beach as well. She had borrowed a friend's van so that she could drive us both to the airport the next day.

Early the next morning, with both sadness and joy in my heart at everything I'd experienced over the past two amazing months on the Hawaiian islands, we packed up and hiked up the same narrow trail I'd hiked down seven weeks earlier, though it felt much more like a lifetime. We piled into her van and drove south down the coast towards the airport, as the sun shone down through scattered clouds, to journey home.

Chapter 17

When dealing with the authorities, try to keep your clothes on (June 1998)

Another summer later, I was back in Hawaii, once again on the beautiful Na Pali Coast. It had been a long, winding and challenging year of traveling since my last visit to Kauai. After coming back from Hawaii I'd spent that summer at a spiritual community in northern Montana; and then visited another later in the fall in New Mexico. Both of them were interesting and valuable learning experiences, but not quite what I was seeking long-term.

I'd ended up back in the redwoods of northern California that fall, where I lived for a month in my tent through part of an El Nino rainy season. In desperate need for a change at that point, I'd bought another round-trip ticket to Hawaii in the depths of winter, direct to Kauai this time. I arrived on the island with $30 to my name.

First I hiked out to Kauai for a few weeks. Then I fortuitously found a job living and working on a communal organic farm on the north shore, near Kileaua and Secrets Beach. As the time rolled around for my return flight in April, I decided to skip it and stay in Hawaii, since I'd happened upon a pretty good thing with the farm. As spring turned to summer, I was still working on the farm with indefinite future plans (no surprise there). I decided to take a couple of weeks off from toiling away in the dirt, and headed back out to the Kalapani Valley for a break.

I hiked the harrowing eleven miles from the trailhead into the valley, staying a night at the abandoned ranger shack as usual. Upon arriving at the end of the trail, I set up my tent at one of the official campsites in the beachside camping area, near the pristine waterfall that poured down the sheer, rocky cliffs. Things were a little different from the last time I'd been there. As it was now summer, it was warmer and drier, the main beach was much larger due to the shifting tides, and the waves were considerably smaller, since winter was always big wave season. There were also more regular tourists around and less young travelers such as myself.

And, as I was about to find out, the park rangers were more vigilant during summertime about checking campers for valid permits. Though I'd heard this was the case, I was just hoping they wouldn't happen to pop in during the two weeks I was there—since, of course, I didn't have anything resembling permission from the designated authorities.

Blissfully ignorant of the forthcoming drama, I set up camp, kicked back and relaxed as I allowed it to soak in that I had, once again, arrived at this rare treasure of a place. I spent the next few days lying on the beach, swimming in the mellow waves, reading in my hammock, going for day hikes up into the valley to pick fruit, showering in the waterfall by the beach and generally enjoying myself. Since there weren't too many other fellow travelers around this time, I pretty much kept to myself. I was figuring to stay down by the beach for the first week, then move my camp farther up into the valley for the second week, just for a change of scene.

On the third or fourth day, I was greeted with a rude awakening. It was early afternoon and I was hanging out naked on the beach, my sarong and a book lying in the sand nearby. I decided to go for a walk in the buff a little ways down the beach. Just as I was about to head into the water to cool off, I happened to glance up—to see what looked like a military commando unit hiking in single-file about a quarter-mile down the main trail, coming towards the camping area and the beach.

The park rangers never hike the entire eleven-mile trail out to the Kalapani Valley. They always helicopter in (and they are the only ones allowed to fly in), landing either at a helicopter pad right by the beach or else another landing pad a half-mile up the trail, if they want the element of surprise. When I was there during winter, a couple of low-key maintenance people had flown in a few times to restock toilet paper in the outhouses, take out some garbage and that was pretty much it. They hadn't bothered to check anyone for camping permits.

But I'd heard stories about the state park rangers, who had quite a different mission entirely. Their duties were, firstly, to politely check the permits of those who were legitimately camped in the designated areas; and secondly, to seek out and find those who were not legitimate tourists but instead hippies or other nudist, freaky weirdoes trying to commune with nature, or some other strangeness (such as yours truly) and send them back to the so-called real world to pay a fine, or perhaps even have a chat with a judge if they'd been cited before. They not only checked the campground by the beach, but also hiked way up into the valley in groups, searching out people living illegally back in the jungle.

Now let me just say that I don't necessarily consider myself right or wrong to be camping on public land without a permit. I just do what I do, try to enjoy myself while making a point not to harm others, learn a little something along the way (or oftentimes learn a lot) and do my best to take responsibility for my actions. I understand that the toilet paper-installers and permit-checkers need to make a living. I also understand that too many people and their corresponding footprints (literally and figuratively) can have an adverse affect on the natural environment.

But really, it's too many *disrespectful* or ignorant people who can adversely affect the environment. If people feel so fond of nature that they actually want to go out and live there, then in my opinion they should pretty much be allowed to do so in this supposedly free country of ours. Thirty-thousand people gathered together in the woods at a Rainbow Gathering, for example, does far less damage to the forest than a handful of people armed with saws and logging trucks, or even a small group of people recreating who leave their garbage behind and pollute the area. A few dozen people living in a valley in the Hawaiian jungle is pretty much how people did things for thousands of years. Smelly, naked people camped out in the woods aren't the ones posing a serious threat to our overburdened planet. It's okay to leave some footprints on the land. Humans will always impact the land they live on. But it was clear to me that the impact those of us were having on the Kalapani Valley by staying there for a few week or months, was nothing remotely detrimental to the natural cycles of nature. But these guys marching single-file down the path in my direction, who had apparently flown to the landing pad a half-mile down the trail, so as to catch folks such as myself off-guard in their birthday suits—didn't resonate much with all that airy-fairy, Mother-Earthy mumbo-jumbo. They were there to enforce the law, hand out tickets, and that was that. As soon as I saw them coming, I realized who they were and knew that I had to think fast to deal with the situation, one way or another; or else my pleasant respite away from work would be sadly and abruptly cut short.

I quickly turned around and started walking back down the beach to get my sarong, so that whatever might happen next at least I would be somewhat covered up. As soon as I started walking back in the other direction, I heard a shout from down the trail behind me. I turned my head, and one of the commando men was running down the trail. Soon enough he was out on the beach and trudging through the sand after me, yelling at me to stop immediately, as if I were armed and dangerous. I just kept walking until I came to my sarong and then wrapped it around my waist. Right about then he came running up to me.

"What do you think you're doing—trying to get away from

me?" he yelled. "Can't you hear? I told you to stop walking."

"I wasn't trying to get away from you. I was just coming to get my sarong so that I could put it on."

When I said that, he calmed down a little.

"Alright buddy…Well, let me see your camping permit, then."

"Sorry man, I don't have one."

"Okay then, I'm writing you up. A fifty-dollar fine, and you'll have to leave the valley immediately," he said with apparent satisfaction. "Now, what's your name and social security number? And I'm going to need to see some ID."

I quickly concocted a story. "You see, the thing is that I don't have my ID on me, because I'm actually camped a couple of miles back down the trail. I just hiked down here to the beach in my sarong for a quick swim."

"Alright, well…" he said, visibly perturbed, since he couldn't very well ask that I take him to my supposed camp, miles away. "Name and social security number, then."

I gave him a fake name and number. He wrote up a ticket, handed it to me and stated gruffly, "Now, we're going to be camped out here for the next two or three days. I better not see you around here again, or you just might get yourself a free helicopter ride back to Lihue. Trust me, you don't want that."

I took the ticket and walked up the beach, pretending I was headed to the campground's restroom. Then I walked quickly back to my nearby campsite. I hurriedly began packing up my camp, hoping that the same ranger wouldn't come across me before I got the hell out of there—as well as wondering what I was going to do for the next two days, while the park ranger commando unit was hanging out and scouring the place.

I was able to take down my tent and hammock and pack up without any further hassle. I strapped on my loaded backpack and started walking down the trail out of the campground—tossing my ticket in a garbage can along the way. I was thinking of hiking a couple miles down the trail to camp at the eight-mile-mark, away from the fray for the next few days until the rangers were gone. Then I could come back to enjoy another week, knowing that they wouldn't be coming back anytime soon, having just done the valley sweep. I really didn't feel like leaving the valley at all. But I seemed to have little choice.

As I was on my way down the trail, about a half-mile past the campground, I noticed a faint path going up a steep embankment to the top of a bluff, which led straight into some thick bushes. I remembered this was the place called the Honeymoon Suite, where a campsite was cleared out in the bushes that overlooked the ocean. I glanced around to make sure no one was watching; and then climbed up the hill and disappeared into the thick cover of bushes.

I had only been up there once before, over a year earlier. There was a small but cozy little clearing in the bushes, completely invisible from the main trail below. And previously unknown to me, the path continued on from there further into the bushes. I decided to follow it and see if there were more campsites. The narrow path continued for a ways, and the bushes eventually turned into a bamboo forest. The path became like a tunnel through the bamboo, which eventually led to another small clearing, and then another, and yet another. The last clearing was the most concealed, as well as the roomiest. I decided to call it home and hope that the rangers didn't know about this spot. I set down my backpack with a sigh of relief and started setting up my new, hopefully secret camp.

I spent the next two long, anxiety-ridden days hiding from and dodging the rangers. They never did search the Honeymoon Suite where I was camped. But I could hear them regularly traversing the trail at the bottom of the hill below me, as they made their way up into the valley to root out squatters hiding back in the jungle.

If I'd been extra cautious, then I would have stayed hidden safely at my campsite deep in the bushes until the rangers left the valley for good. I had everything I needed right there, other than water, which I could have gotten from a nearby creek under cover of night. But it got a little boring after half a day just sitting around my camp. And besides it was too enticing not to play a little hide-and-seek with the rangers, since that seemed to be the game they liked to play.

So I ventured away from my camp in the bushes every once in a while and kept my ears open for their loud voices and footsteps coming down the path. I even got so bold as to sit out in the sun a little ways off the path and read a book, near some bushes for cover—being careful to listen for the rangers stumbling in my direction. When I did hear any voices or footsteps, I leapt into a nearby bush and waited for them to pass.

Once, one of the rangers apparently caught a glimpse of me, because two or three of them started combing the area around where I was hiding. I'd managed to hide myself deep in a huge bush, amidst a cluster of other bushes. They never did find me. But for a good thirty minutes or so, which felt like a heck of a long time, I was trapped in a bush as the rangers went back and forth over the entire area looking for me. These guys were tenacious, and took their work seriously.

The following day, once again bored of hanging out at my campsite, I decided to venture farther up into the valley. I took a route going from my hidden campsite directly through the jungle, so as to stay off the trail as much as possible. Eventually I came across the main trail, about a mile up the valley. I listened carefully for any voices, but could hear nothing other than a few birds chirping away. So I continued walking stealthily up the path, stopping every once in a while to listen for the rangers.

I was just about to hop over a little creek flowing across the path, when I heard a sudden movement in the jungle. I looked up—and saw someone about twenty feet up the creek, partly hidden in the shadows. We both instantly froze. I looked closer, and then realized that she, almost naked with long, dark brown dreadlocks, definitely wasn't a park ranger. Whoever she was, she must have simultaneously realized the same about me, because she stepped out of the shadows a little so that I could see her better. At that point we recognized one other.

"Heather?" I said. She was a friend who lived near the farm, and visited occasionally, and was also one of the folks who had taken part in the full moon sweat lodge ceremony the previous year. And, she happened to be one of the most beautiful women I've ever known.

"Gabriel? God, I'm glad to see it's you. I thought at first you were another ranger." She came walking alongside the creek towards me.

"How's it going?" I said. "I didn't know you were out here. Have you managed to avoid the rangers?"

"Not completely," she said, as she walked up and gave me a hug. "Let's go somewhere safe where we can talk, and I'll tell you all about it."

"How about my camp? I'm down at the Honeymoon Suite. It seems pretty well hidden. I don't think the rangers know about it, or they would have been there by now."

"That sounds great. How do we get there without getting caught? I can't afford another ticket." She'd had a run-in with the rangers already herself.

We made it slowly back to my camp by picking our way through the forest, staying off the main path. Then she relayed to me how she'd been surprised by the rangers while she was down at the creek getting water. She had been fasting, and had no idea that the rangers had flown in. All of a sudden, she looked up from the creek while filling her water bottle and three big rangers were standing there staring at her. She was caught totally off guard, especially since she was in a hypersensitive state from fasting—and her mind ran wild with all the frightening explanations for what they were doing there. But soon enough she figured out who they were. They wrote her up the same 50 dollar ticket that I had gotten, made her go get her ID (thus revealing her camp to them) and then forced her to pack up her things and march down the trail. Once she was out of their sight and they'd moved on up the valley, she doubled back and found herself another, better concealed campsite. She'd been totally freaked when she first saw me, because she thought she was about to replay the whole unsettling scenario, and was kicking herself for getting caught again.

We spent the rest of that afternoon hanging out at my campsite, conversing as quietly as possible. Later in the evening, she asked if she could move her camp down next to mine, so that she wouldn't have to worry about the rangers for the next day or so before they left. I said sure, I didn't mind at all. If anything I was starved for some company. She decided to go back up into the valley right away, to pack up her things and bring them down. The rangers seemed to have quit their searching for the day as evening descended, since we hadn't heard them along the trail below my camp for a while. They were most likely back at the campground, cooking up burgers, drinking beer and telling jokes about the freak hippies they'd chased out of various parts of the jungle that day.

Heather left and I got a small fire started to cook dinner. About an hour later, she came back down the path through the bamboo forest. She set down her pack with a huge sigh of relief for having made it back safely. Then she set up her own little tent next door, where there was another small clearing in the bushes adjacent to mine, almost like a guest room. Afterwards she came over to join me by the fire, and we sat before the flames, talking and cooking up the usual rice and lentils.

The rangers finally flew out late the next morning. No longer needing the element of surprise, their helicopter roared noisily overhead, going first from one helicopter pad to the other to load up all the troops. Eventually it lifted off and sputtered away. The two of us just looked at each other and smiled, as we were finally left in the peace and silence of nature, as it was meant to be.

Heather and I had some great adventures and conversations together over the next few days. In addition to being attractive, easygoing and earthy, she was also incredibly intelligent and engaging. We continued camping in the same spot at the Honeymoon Suite. Now that the rangers were gone, we were ever so grateful for the freedom to carry on without fear as we enjoyed the exquisite beauty of the valley.

We went skinny-dipping in the ocean or the valley creek, did yoga on the bluffs, went for hikes up into the valley, bathed in the waterfall, cooked up hearty meals together in the evenings and, like I said, had great conversations. We managed to cover just about every topic conceivable—from philosophy to food, spirituality, love, sex, movies, writing, men, women, physics, astronomy, astrology, dreams, failures and anything else that happened to cross our minds or hearts.

We had a blast spending precious, priceless time together, sharing stories and lazy days. Heather was easy to get along with. She was a woman who seemed to know how to handle her feminine allure. She was neither stuck-up about it, nor overly reserved. She was empowered without lacking humility. She was confident, but not cold and distant. She was mysterious without being inaccessible. I could totally relate to her, even as I was practically knocked off my feet just being around her. She neither flaunted nor hid her feminine being. She was a genuine creature of love and beauty, and I enjoyed just being around her open and forthright humanness.

Needless to say, I was sad when she left. I planned to stay in the valley for another five days or so on my own before heading back to work on the farm. But there's really nothing more a person can ask for in life than that rare and unique occasion when two people totally click together—whether for a few days or a lifetime, you're lucky if it happens at all. I knew I would likely see her again around the island, and maybe even back on the mainland sometime, somewhere. And I knew also that it probably wouldn't be quite the same...But then, I guess it never really is the same, is it?

Part 5

India, 1999-2000

Chapter 18

A rupee is only worth a rupee
(October 1999)

I arrived in New Delhi, India after four flights and two layovers totaling thirty-six hours, totally exhausted and bordering on delirious. I never could sleep much on planes or buses, other than occasional brief, sporadic moments of semi-unconsciousness from sheer delirium, that only managed to make the experience even more surreal. And I'd been too anxious and excited the night before flying to sleep well either. So I'd gotten altogether perhaps five hours of sleep in the last forty-eight. It was evening when we finally touched ground on Indian soil, just getting dark, and all I could think about was dragging myself to a bed somewhere to crash.

A friend who previously traveled to India had prepared me somewhat for my arrival in New Delhi, including what I should reasonably pay for a taxi into the city—around 200 *rupees*, or about five U.S. dollars. Once I'd made it through customs, I changed some dollars into rupees, and then walked over to the taxi reservation area.

There were two kiosks for two different taxi companies on either side of a long, wide walkway leading out of the airport. Behind each reservation desk was a boisterous group of Indian men. They all immediately began hollering and waving at me as I approached, to come to their window and give them my business. After a moment of indecision I settled on the group that seemed slightly less pushy, and walked over to them.

"How much for a taxi to Paharganj?" I inquired. Paharganj is a popular travelers marketplace in Delhi, where many of the cheap hotels are located, and is conveniently located right near the New Delhi Railway Station. (New Delhi is the part of Delhi that was constructed by the British during their occupation of India.) My friend had recommended a hotel in that area for my stay in Delhi. He'd also warned me not to get sucked into the taxi drivers attempts to take you to other, more expensive hotels, for whom they worked and would get paid commission.

"Two-hundred fifty rupees," he said.

Close enough. I was way too tired to haggle over fifty rupees right then, or one American dollar.

"Can you take me to the Vivek Hotel?" I asked.

"Vivek? Sure, no problem. You pay now, and go out front. Your taxi will be waiting—this is your driver," he said, gesturing at another man standing beside him, who flashed me a big smile and then gave a customary Indian bobble of the head.

I paid the fare and walked towards the front doors of the airport, where he'd indicated I should wait for the driver. On my way out I passed a long line of Indians waiting for arrivals, who all stared at my backpack and me as curiously and intently as if I were a two-headed monkey in a circus sideshow. Welcome to India—time to get used to being an object of curiosity.

After standing outside the airport for about ten minutes, starting to feel not unlike a monkey, wondering if I'd already been scammed in the course of my first transaction, a small white sedan pulled up abruptly and I recognized the driver as the man from the taxi window. He gave me a big, enthusiastic grin again, and then got out to open the rear trunk for my backpack. He gestured towards the door—passenger on the left, driver on the right, same arrangement as the British Isles. We both clambered in and then abruptly zipped off, leaving the airport, and much of the 20th century, far behind.

Though I'd been under the impression on my arrival that the airport seemed a little forsaken and run-down, this thought quickly changed in contrast to the garbage-strewn, chaotic streets of Delhi. If my arrival in London years earlier had felt like stepping out of an elevator onto another planet, the harsh reality of India was more like an alternate dimension.

Despite everything I'd heard beforehand, all the crazy stories from other travelers, all the photo books I'd perused, I was still unprepared for the stark change of reality, of consciousness, of humanity that is India. It felt much like time traveling into the past, or perhaps like an odd, jumbled mixture of past, present and future. But even more evident than the technological shift backwards, which was striking but expected, was a cultural shift from the Western world that was difficult to grasp. The sheer numbers of people and vehicles on the streets was unlike anything in Western cities. There was so much sensory input going on all at once that I could hardly figure out how to process it.

The traffic became extremely congested as we neared the main part of the city. And yet there were no dividing lines on the pavement to separate the five or six lanes of traffic. Puttering old mopeds zipped between the cars carrying entire families of four or five. Young children wove through the cluttered lines of traffic at intersections, begging at the stopped cars, including a girl, perhaps eight or nine, who came to our vehicle in a stained white dress with a dirty face, stringy dark hair and sparkling, vibrant, haunting brown eyes. The driver ignored her as if she were a ghost. When she came around to my side of the car I just smiled and waved a little, feeling a mix of guilt, compassion and the overarching exhaustion that left me unable to react to much of anything right then. I considered reaching into my pocket and sifting through my wad of cash to hand her something. But before that could happen we were on our way again, weaving through the turbulent maelstrom of a still-developing civilization.

Cows were lying halfway in the road, undisturbed by the constant commotion around them. Monkeys swung from tattered trees that hung out over the traffic, their frenzied activity eerily lit by randomly placed and flickering street lamps. Many of the city streets were unpaved, and none of the scattered stoplights seemed to be working. The drivers managed to avoid hitting one another by some means of subtle communication entirely beyond my comprehension. And since there were no crosswalks, people crossed the street simply by putting out their hand as a signal to keep from being run over, then launching casually into the clogged stream of traffic.

Thinking back on it, the taxi ride that night was a frenetic, overwhelming blur of unfamiliar cultural immersion that altogether bewildered my clouded, sleepy consciousness. It was like trying to watch TV when there were three different channels all superimposed on top of one another. It was just too much to try to sort out.

And yet on some other level, once you let go of the expectation of understanding what was going on, instead surrendering to the very different flow of life and adjusting your perceptions, it almost seemed as if this mad jumble of assorted chaos managed to work together in a method of orderliness. It was just different. Way different. And as it became clear that my driver was perfectly capable of making it through the pandemonium, despite my apprehension, I did my best just to sit back, relax and go with the flow, and trust that it would all work itself out one way or another...though not without a detour here and there.

At one point, the driver managed to communicate in his limited English that he needed some clearer directions to the hotel, and he was going to stop by a local travel office to call and ask. Hoping to avoid any further delays on the route to my bed, I pulled out my travel book, which indicated clearly on a city map where the hotel was located. I held the page up to him, and he briefly glanced at it.

"No, no, that's no good," he said. "I ask, no problem—you will see." I had a flash of impending complications, as my friend's warning of conniving taxi drivers came quickly to mind.

Soon he pulled down a narrow side street and parked in front of a dilapidated structure that vaguely resembled an office of some kind, only because of a sign out front that said "Office Tourists. Speaking English." My driver told me to wait just a minute. He got out of the car and went inside. After a few minutes he came back out and informed me that the Vivek Hotel was full. This was precisely the scenario my friend had outlined in my pre-departure briefing.

"I know very nice hotel I can take you," he said. "Deluxe room, TV, good price—you will like."

"You called the Vivek?" I asked.

"Yes, all full."

"I want to talk to them myself," I said.

He looked at me a little disgruntled, and then told me to come inside with him. A man was sitting at a small desk with a telephone, looking bored and unpleasant. My driver rattled off something in Hindi, and the man picked up the phone and dialed. He talked quickly to someone at the other end, then handed me the receiver.

"Vivek Hotel?" I said.

"Yes," said a voice at the other end of the line.

"Do you have any rooms available for tonight?" I asked.

"Rooms? No, all full. Sorry, very busy."

I realized then that I was too exhausted to push it any further. No doubt the guy at the other end of the line was a friend of theirs, nowhere near my intended hotel. I hung up the phone and told the driver to take me to the place he had in mind.

We drove through more winding streets and tangled masses of traffic for a while longer, as I drifted in and out of consciousness; before finally pulling up in front of the Ivory Palace Resort. I retrieved my pack from the trunk, and the driver followed me up the shiny marble steps to the reception area, no doubt to collect his share of the spoils.

"How much for a room?" I asked at the front desk.

The nicely dressed man looked me over for just an instant, before saying, "Eight hundred rupees."

I knew this was rather outrageous. My friend had told me before leaving that the mid-range Vivek Hotel would be around 200 rupees—and that was the most I should reasonably pay for a decent room in India. I asked to see the room, and the bellboy took me up three flights of spiraling stairs. It was undoubtedly luxurious by Indian standards, with a double bed, tiled bathroom with hot water, air-conditioning and a small refrigerator. I figured they were still jacking the price on me, even for this. Eight hundred rupees was about twenty American dollars. Multiply that by ten (most things in India run about a tenth the Western price), and you have the equivalent Indian price—200 dollars. The room was nice. But not that nice.

But I was a newly-arrived foreigner in a strange and distant land, and it was all unfamiliar and overwhelming, and they knew it. The double bed was beckoning. And it wasn't a fortune. I could afford to splurge my first few days, even if it bruised my ego a little. I walked back downstairs to check in. I couldn't be bothered to attempt to haggle, and save at most a few dollars. I registered and forked over the 800 rupees, feeling somehow as if it were 800 bucks. Then I walked back upstairs to my room, locked the door, took a long, hot shower (admiring the tiled blue floor in my sleep-deprived daze), crawled into the wide, fairly cozy bed...and promptly crashed.

I awoke mid-morning to the constant, cluttered sounds of India emanating from beyond my clouded mind. I would have liked to have stayed there through the day, soak up the deluxe amenities and not have to bother moving. But I was on a squeaky tight budget for the next five months of around ten dollars per day, and didn't want to lose control of my wallet right off the bat. I packed up, headed out and got another taxi to the Paharganj district.

I easily found the Vivek Hotel, which wasn't at all full. I checked in and paid the 200 rupees, grumbling a little for allowing myself to be swindled my first day in India, despite the ample warning. I spent the rest of the day exploring the extensive Paharganj marketplace, buying some clothes and other traveling items at starkly cheap prices, even before attempting to bring them down a little. Despite the backwardness of the filthy Indian streets, ever-present beggars and solemn cows hanging around chewing on cardboard and plastic bags, it seemed you could get almost anything you might need or want at one of the many small shops, specializing in everything from incense to stereo equipment. The exotic marketplace was like a vast candy store for budget travelers. In fact, there were even several candy stores, and I experimented with a few tasty Indian sweets.

My plan from Delhi was to head first to the small mountain town of Rishikesh, in the foothills of the Himalaya and along the Ganges River. My friend had recommended it as a good place to get acquainted with India, without being entirely overwhelmed by it. I figured I'd stay there for a week or two, do some yoga in one of the many ashrams along the river, hopefully meet up with some fellow travelers and get a little more comfortable traversing this intense and mysterious land; before venturing onward for the rest of my five-month journey.

Chapter 19

Hold onto your chai
(November 1999)

I wish I could say now that I'd actually hitchhiked in India. The only thing is that I never, for a second, actually wanted to *be* hitchhiking while I was there. I met folks who had done it—on little mountain roads winding through the Himalaya, where they were picked up and tossed, along with their luggage, onto the rack on top; and then held on for dear life as the bus brushed under tree limbs and careened around hairpin corners, skirting cliffs that dropped down a thousand feet or more. Just riding the bus the usual way in India was more excitement than I was generally in the mood for. The highway system over there is nothing short of chaos.

Imagine this: You're on a rickety old bus somewhere between two major Indian cities, flying down a decrepit two-lane highway (pretty much the only kind of road they have, to varying degrees of decrepitation). You come, as usual, to a long line of buses and large trucks lined up behind one another as they lumber along, slowed down by a vehicle in the front of the line. Your bus driver happens to be the type who drank a little too much chai at the last rest stop—nothing out of the ordinary, but you sense that his judgment and sense of distance may be impaired ever so slightly.

He pulls out to pass the long row of vehicles. Immediately, you see another large truck coming at you a ways down the highway. This doesn't seem to concern your driver in the slightest. He just keeps on barreling down the opposing lane, creeping sluggishly past the first, second, third and then fourth vehicle.

Nearing the fifth and second-to-last vehicle in the line, the truck coming at you is now alarmingly close—much too close for your own bus to clear the end of the line and find its proper lane. Your stomach starts to wrench with acute distress.

And then, with a sudden, horrifying realization of impending cataclysm, you realize that, in addition to this already distressing scenario, the truck coming down the road towards you is *also* being passed by a hasty and manic bus driver in its improper lane. Neither does this undeniable absurdity concern your driver terribly.

There are now two parallel lanes of traffic both filled with vehicles going in opposing directions—the only reasonable outcome here being a catastrophic, head-on pile-up. None of the vehicles are slowing down at all. The people seated around you are all eerily comatose. You're on the verge of leaping out of your seat, running to the front of the bus to grab a hold of the steering wheel and career the rig off into the barren landscape to avoid certain doom. But then, something miraculous occurs in the course of a few split seconds.

Your bus driver casually sticks his arm out the window, signaling to the truck he's just passing—who then puts on his brakes a little, creating barely enough space between him and the truck at the front of the line. At the last possible instant, your bus suddenly pulls over into its rightful lane, sliding in between the two vehicles. The other bus coming in your direction simultaneously whips in front of the truck that it was passing, flying through the space you were just occupying only milliseconds before. The two rows of vehicles then manage to glide smoothly past one another without incident, everything clicking together in magical unison like a colossal and terrifying game of highway Tetris.

No one else on the bus would be having the same heart-pounding, near-death experience as yourself. They would just be sitting there calmly, snacking on peanuts or fussing with their children or whatever, since that was pretty much a routine Indian bus ride event (especially in the more populated north, where the roads are extremely overloaded).

After my first month of taking buses in India, I made a point of taking the trains whenever possible. Not only were they much safer and less nerve-wracking, but they were also a hell of a lot more comfortable. And whenever I did happen to ride the bus, I would sit way in the back so that I couldn't see what was happening in the road ahead. Sometimes ignorance is indeed bliss (or at least better than abject terror). I would also hold my backpack on my lap, between myself and the back of the seat in front of me, as some sort of minimal protection in case the seemingly inevitable were to happen, and I was suddenly hurled forward in the general direction of my demise.

It's extraordinary that the Indian traffic system works at all. In addition to the highways being insanely jam-packed, they're also shared by everything from the usual buses, trucks and passenger cars, to farmers on puttering tractors, ox-drawn carts, cocky young men on motorcycles, bicycles, pedestrians, the occasional camel or elephant, and of course the ever-present sacred cows, standing wherever they please. Somehow, this barrage of moving vehicles and bodies manages to coexist without causing total mayhem.

I'm reminded of a piece of trivia that my friend Abram (the one I shaved my eyebrows with) once proclaimed authoritatively (which he liked to do often). Whether true or not, it makes a point. Large bumblebees are able to fly, not because their wingspan/bodyweight ratio actually supports them, but simply because they believe, without question, that they should be able to. The Indian roadways and the country in general similarly seems to work not because it makes any practical, rational, realistic sense; but because the people living there have little choice other than to assume that things will somehow work themselves out, if they're going to get anything at all accomplished in their overpopulated, overburdened, oxymoronic country.

Chapter 20

Get good directions on the way to the rainbow (December 1999)

I rolled into the small town of Gokarna—in Karnataka State on the Arabian Sea along India's western coast—concluding a typically harrowing day-long bus ride. At least in this less-populated region of India the bus journeys weren't quite so death-defying as simply highly unpleasant. Or maybe I was just getting numb to the peril from my past two months of traveling.

Immediately after stepping off the bus, a man was standing there, offering a room for the night. The price was dirt cheap at 80 rupees (less than two dollars) and he was extremely gracious, so I agreed to take a look. I followed him out of the bus station and through the small, tranquil village towards his hotel. Dusk was settling, and I was more than ready to lay down my head. Even when not fearing for your life, the Indian buses can be exhausting, just trying to stay on your seat. The drawback of my defensive move of sitting at the back of the bus was that it put me where it was most sensitive to the incongruities of the road.

It turned out, as is often the case, that his "hotel" was actually a couple of small rooms attached to the outside of his own house—otherwise known as a guesthouse. Guesthouses can sometimes be nicer than regular hotels, especially in terms of hospitality, since they are often run by a friendly family, rather than a handful of money-grubbing men. The room was sparse but clean, so I agreed to his reasonable price. He then showed me to the squat toilet and bucket shower for later use.

I was in the village of Gokarna because of rumors of a Rainbow Gathering I'd heard about earlier in my trip, which was supposedly happening somewhere in this area around New Year's. I was rather surprised to learn that a Rainbow Gathering was happening in India. Though I knew they were a worldwide phenomenon, they took place mostly in Western countries, so it hadn't occurred to me that they might take place here. Apparently they were actually organized by foreign travelers, and then word was spread via the traveler's grapevine. I'd heard about this one from some friends in India who had sent me an email. Though I'd known I would be in India for New Year's Y2K, I hadn't known exactly where I would end up for the much-hyped occasion. A Rainbow Gathering sounded like the best place to be, especially if the modern, technological world indeed came to a screeching halt. In that case, we would hardly notice…at least until we headed back to town to stock up on supplies.

So I'd kept it in mind over the past couple of months, as I made my way south from Rishikesh in the Himalayan foothills, to see the exquisite Taj Mahal in Agra; wandered through the deserts of Rajasthan; explored the squalid metropolis of Bombay; and finally immersed myself in the invigorating waters of the Arabian Coast in the state of Goa, just north of Gokarna. Now that I was here, I just had to find out where this Rainbow Gathering was taking place—if indeed it still was.

The small spiritual town of Gokarna had become popular with travelers in recent years, due to its three secluded nearby beaches. To get to them, you had to hike a little ways along a trail across some bluffs overlooking the coast, coming after about a half-mile to the first beach. At the end of that beach, a trail continued up and over the cliffs to the next beach. From there, the trail continued to yet another beach—one called Om Beach because of its graceful curves remarkably resembling the Indian *om* symbol (which refers, more or less, to the spiritual hum of the universe).

I stayed that night in my small but pleasant room at the guesthouse, sleeping intermittently due to the usual thin Indian mattress, as well as a plethora of pesky mosquitoes. The next morning I got up early, went for breakfast at a local restaurant, then hiked out of town to check out the beaches and see what signs of the gathering I could find. In the email my friend had sent me, the word was that the gathering would likely be somewhere near Om Beach. I stopped to swim at each of the other two beaches along the way, and did some bodysurfing in the gentle waves. It was a typically sunny and warm winter day in India (winter is their dry season—in my five months in India I saw only a few cloudy days, and virtually no rain). The water was pleasantly refreshing, keeping me cool for my hike across the headlands between the beaches.

I finally made it to Om Beach, with no apparent sign of the Rainbow Gathering. The gatherings draw a pretty distinctive crowd of freakish hippie-types, easily identifiable, and from what I'd heard people should have been in the process of setting it up by now. But all I came across were the usual young budget tourists, sunning themselves in the sand in ones and twos. I also realized that this wouldn't have been a very good place for the Rainbow Gathering to take place anyway—not enough open space away from the beach, and not enough privacy. The gatherings don't work well with too many random people wandering through, stopping by inquisitively just to see what was going on.

I left Om Beach and headed back towards town, feeling a bit sad and dejected, assuming that the gathering must have been cancelled for some reason or another. Whoever had come up with the original idea had probably come down here to scope it out and then concluded, as I did, that it wasn't a prime place for a gathering after all. Or maybe they'd simply followed a whim to another part of India, or another country, and abandoned the idea altogether.

I hiked the trail back into town to find some dinner and think about what to do next. I figured that I'd at least hang around the area for a few more days, enjoy the beaches and see if anything else came up, before moving on. Perhaps I would come across a few other travelers looking for the gathering, and we could put something together on our own.

I arrived back in town late in the afternoon and walked up the dusty main street, checking out the different restaurants for a good, cheap *thali* (basic Indian meal including rice, vegetable dishes and *chapati*, the Indian version of a tortilla). As I was standing in front of one of the restaurants, mulling over their menu, I heard a shout from across the street aimed in my general direction.

"Hey man! You want to go to a Rainbow Gathering?"

I looked back, and there was a small group of scraggly, smiling young folks seated at the outdoor table of another restaurant, drinking banana *lassis* (an Indian yogurt drink).

I walked over to them, feeling a gaggle of butterflies fluttering in my empty stomach with anticipation of encouraging news that it was still happening.

"Yeah, definitely! That's what I've been looking around for. Do you guys know something about it?" I asked.

"Sure thing, we just came into town from the site—it's just getting started a ways up the coast, about fifteen miles. It's an amazing spot. We can give you directions, but they're a little hard to follow. You'll have to take a bus to another small village and then do some walking. But you can just ask the locals along the way if you get lost, and they'll point you in the right direction."

I joined the small group for a lassi myself, and wrote down the convoluted directions, with instructions along the lines of "take a left at the big bush" and "turn right at the little trail". It sounded like a perfect recipe for confusion.

Two of the travelers were from Germany, one was from Canada and another was a "Kiwi", from New Zealand. They filled me in on the happenings at the gathering site, as we all slurped on our smoothies in the warm sunshine. The gathering had gotten underway a few days earlier, although New Year's was still over a week away. A small group of a dozen or so were there now building "seed camp", getting the site prepared for the many folks who would undoubtedly be arriving soon. They said it was a small, beautiful and secluded beach, the only potential drawback being that some were concerned it might not be adequate for a large crowd. Hopefully word hadn't spread too terribly far and wide.

Soon they had to leave to catch their bus up the coast towards the gathering. I thanked them for the well-timed information, and told them I'd probably see them out there the next day. I spent that night again at the mosquito-infested guesthouse. The next morning I bought some food and other provisions at the local market, packed up and headed out, directions firmly in hand.

Of course I got lost along the way. Following the scribbled directions, I caught the local bus about ten miles up the coast to a tiny, tiny village situated on a wide, dark and sluggish river that flowed into the ocean, which was just a few miles away from that point. Another speck of a village rested on the opposite bank of the river. It was from that village that the apparent hike to the gathering site began. A small motorboat took the villagers (and their groceries, chickens, cows, motorcycles and other necessities of life) back and forth across the river for a few rupees. On the short ferry ride I met up with another traveler, an older man from the U.K. named Bruce, who was also headed for the gathering and had his own set of vague directions. We decided to put our heads together, as well as our maps, and between the two of us hopefully find our way out there fairly smoothly.

But as they'd warned the previous day, the directions were indeed hard to follow. I guess the quest for the rainbow isn't meant to be a straight line. We got off the ferry on the other side of the river, and strolled through the small Indian village. The local townsfolk peered at us with a mix of both curiosity and wariness, as if they'd hardly seen a fair-skinned person in their lives. And even if they had, it probably wasn't in their little out-of-the-way village. The larger nearby town of Gokarna had been relatively unknown by foreigners until just a few years before. But this much smaller village was completely off the map, tourist or otherwise. The only thing bringing us travelers out there was a small, isolated beach a few miles away—which, I found out later, had been discovered quite fortuitously by a persistent German man who had wandered well off the beaten path in his search for a suitable gathering site.

From the village, the two of us hiked along a well-used path beside the river, heading west towards the ocean. After a half-mile or so we came to a small clay schoolhouse, which both of our directions mentioned. So far, so good. A dozen or so school children were outside and they converged on the two of us immediately, hollering for the usual sought-after items of foreign coins, pens, candy and of course rupees. We smiled and said hello and "Namaste" a number of times. Then we did our best to politely ignore them and their insistent demands as they coagulated around us, and tried to make sense of our directions. The path branched off into three different, fainter trails from the schoolhouse. But it turned out that mine said to go straight— whereas Bruce's seemed to indicate we should go right. Damn.

The teacher was standing at the door of the schoolhouse, watching the noisy spectacle we'd become thanks to the convergence of his own pupils. I remembered what they'd said if I got lost, to ask the locals. I waved hello to the schoolteacher, and he waved back. Then Bruce and I both pointed at two of the possible directions before us and gave him a questioning shrug. He got the message and waved his hand up the small path forward, where my directions had indicated. Whether his assurance that this was the way was because he'd seen other foreigners go that direction, or simply because he wanted to get rid of us, we would find out soon enough. We said thank you, and then said goodbye and "Namaste" again to the crowd of boisterous schoolchildren, and continued hiking from there up the path.

The trail wound through a thick forest of shady, cooling Aspen-like trees. We could tell that we were nearing the ocean, and by our directions that meant (so we assumed) that we were also nearing the gathering. We were both excited to see the beautiful beach we'd heard about, mingle with fellow travelers and take a refreshing swim in the ocean to wash away the dirt, sweat and grime from our hike.

A half-mile or so later, we indeed reached the ocean. Or rather, we reached a steep, rocky cliff that dropped precipitously down to the ocean, at nothing vaguely resembling a beach. We stood there for a few moments in confusion, feeling a conflicting mix of fleeting success and unanticipated defeat.

We'd made it to the coast. But there was no sign of the idyllic beach that had been described the day before, nor any indications of other traveling Westerners nearby. Looking each way up and down the coast, all we could see were more steep, rugged cliffs, with the dense forest coming right up near the edge. It felt not unlike a cruel joke of some kind. In our quest for Arabian Beach Paradise, we'd instead fallen upon the Craggy Cliffs of Despair. Our mirage had faded before we'd even had the chance to witness it.

We decided to take a break at that point and mull over our fate. We hadn't been anticipating quite this much of an adventure, and were already tired out from hiking with our heavily-laden backpacks in the Indian heat. Although, at least I'd learned a thing or two since my travels in Europe ten years earlier, and was carrying a pack about half the size. But it was now overstuffed and cumbersome, packed with a week's worth of food.

We downed ample quantities of water, snacked on some crackers and dates and conferred on what to do from there. We reasoned that, assuming this paradisiacal beach did in fact exist, it must be north of us, since we could still see the mouth of the wide river to the south that we'd just crossed by ferry. And upon taking another look at our flimsy directions, they both seemed to indicate that the beach was further up the coast, perhaps between one of the many ridges that jutted down to the shore.

Finally, mustering some resolve from the bowels of our desperate quest for nirvana, we strapped on our packs again and launched forward into the pathless unknown before us, hoping to heck we were on the right track and might soon witness an enticing mirage off in the distance, which in turn would become reality.

Our guess to head north proved itself right. But it took several hours of ruthless hiking and anxiety-riddled exploring before we actually figured that out. We trudged and scrambled up and down the dusty, rocky coast, climbing embankments and crashing through scratchy bushes in the hot sun, all while the cool ocean waters taunted us far below.

After hours of painfully slow progress, we climbed yet another of many desolate crags, to see off in the distance what looked like a commercial for an exotic beach getaway. Our mirage did exist! About a half-mile up the coast, set between the rocky cliffs, was a pristine sliver of a beach lined with waving palm trees, dotted with tents and naked people strolling through the glimmering white sand and swimming in the pleasantly cascading ocean waves. It seemed far too perfect and beautiful to be true. And yet, to the infinite gratitude of our bedraggled and sweaty bodies, the vision in this case wasn't simply a figment of our despairing and twisted imaginations.

Despite our exhaustion and our leaden packs, Bruce and I both jogged the last stretch of the hike, up and down a few more hills, through a section of forest, up and over a few boulders and then down one final hill to the beach. Once I lumbered onto the sandy beach, I took off my pack, tossed it down, quickly shed my dusty, sweaty clothes, and ran directly into the water. It was an experience of blessed rejuvenation entirely beyond description.

The Rainbow Gathering turned out to be a unique one (as to be expected, given the location). Just thirty or forty people were there most of the time, in stark contrast to the 30,000 people present at the overwhelming national Rainbow Gathering back in the States. The smallest gathering I'd been to previously was my first Oregon regional, with several hundred people. When Bruce and I first stumbled into camp there were only about a dozen people there—though representing almost as many countries.

There was a kitchen area set up at the base of a huge boulder resting on the beach, not far from the breaking waves. That boulder was a godsend, as it provided shade, protection from the wind, something to anchor tarps to and was the perfect backrest to lean against while chopping vegetables, making music or just bullshitting with fellow travelers. Away from the beach was a grove of palm trees and tall bushes that made good camping cover. A small valley led up from the beach area—which, if Bruce and I had been on the right track, we would have come leisurely strolling down after a pleasant hike through the shaded woods.

After my indulgent swim in the ocean, I claimed a good camping spot shaded by the bushes. I wasn't traveling with a tent. But as mentioned it was the dry season and you didn't really need one. It was clear blue, sunny skies almost the whole time I was out there, aside from a few occasional wandering clouds and one brief night-time sprinkle. So I simply spread out a sheet on the sand, tossed my blanket on top of it, scattered a few assorted belongings around and, voila, I was home.

Other than food, which we brought in from Gokarna, we had everything we needed to support us at the gathering site. A freshwater spring flowed out of nearby rocks, which kept us, for the most part, healthy and hydrated. A few people did get sick towards the end of the gathering. Although, of all the different ways to get sick in India, it's hard to say what exactly may have caused it. I drank the spring water every day and didn't have any problems.

A latrine had been dug in the bushes a ways back from the beach. People had brought pots and pans in from town. We cooked up simple meals on a campfire in the beach kitchen area near the large boulder. Blankets were strung up overhead for additional shade during the day. Some were even traveling with instruments, so that we had music as we cooked. During the day we simply lazed about on the beach, swam in the ocean, read books or else did some exploring up the coast.

As the days progressed towards New Year's Eve, more people began to arrive. Though it was primarily Western travelers from Europe, Australia, New Zealand, Israel and the Americas, a handful of Indians found their way there as well, either friends of foreign travelers or others who had simply heard of this unusual event and wanted to see what it was all about.

As people came, and a few left, the vibe of the gathering shifted. Some days it was fun, light and harmonized. Others it was disorganized and discordant as new people, some unfamiliar with the ways of the Rainbow Gatherings, tried to find their place in it—or else tried to turn it into whatever it was they were looking for, such as another wild millennium beach party. Usually, those looking for a good party soon got the idea that this was too mellow to be it, and headed back to the beaches and clubs north in Goa State.

As we approached New Year's Day, the secluded beach started to swell with travelers. Word of the Rainbow Gathering had apparently spread fairly far and wide. Everyone wanted to be somewhere interesting for Y2K. As the gathering became more crowded, growing from a few dozen to eventually several hundred, I started to think that I might rather be elsewhere. Although I also wanted to be somewhere distinctive and memorable for the turning over of the millennium, I didn't want to be cramped and miserable in the process. Having been there a week-and-a-half by that point, I was feeling as if I'd experienced pretty much what I'd come for. I didn't need to stay simply for the sake of being there January 1st, 2000.

I'd made a couple of Israeli friends at the gathering—Yossi and Nadav—who were also feeling a little claustrophobic from the converging crowds. And besides, the energy of the gathering seemed to be slipping from its focused, cooperative, communal beginnings into the beach party that many of the arriving people were looking for.

The day before New Year's Eve, the three of us decided to take off and do our own celebration someplace else. Yossi had read in his guidebook about an area of jungle not far away that was supposedly fairly easy to get to and a good place to camp. We all agreed it sounded like any interesting change of scene.

We packed up early the next morning, December 31st, 1999, hugged goodbye a few friends, then headed up the valley away from the beach and along the narrow, well-worn trail through the woods. At the tiny village by the river, we took the ferryboat across to the other side and then hopped on a bus back to Gokarna.

Chapter 21

A fahking adventure
(New Year's Y2K)

Yossi, Nadav and I spent that morning buying food and other supplies in Gokarna. We figured we'd stay three or four days in the jungle. We stocked up with vegetables, rice, flour for chapatis, tahini, dates, fruit, crackers, spices, cookies and, for celebratory purposes, a cheap bottle of wine.

We then caught a bus from Gokarna to another small village about an hour south along the coast. We hopped one more bus heading inland, up what turned eventually from a narrow road into an even narrower dusty, pot-hole-riddled road choked by encroaching jungle. At that point we were the only ones left on the bus. In the course of a day we were going from a wild beach party on the Arabian sea to a remote region of the Indian jungle. So be it. I was just happy to be on an adventure with a couple of good friends.

Finally we were dropped off at the end of the road at an empty dirt parking lot surrounded entirely by thick jungle. Once the bus had turned around and lumbered back the other way, the only sign of civilization was a little tourist hut selling juice, cookies, bottled water and film. A trail led past the hut and into the jungle. There were no other vehicles and seemed to be no other visitors. After drinking copiously from our own water bottles, we strapped on our backpacks, waved to the bored man at the tourist hut and started hiking up the trail.

Our plans from that point forward were scant, to say the least. We didn't have a map of the area, or tents or even sleeping bags— just a couple of thin blankets each, which had worked fine on the beach and we hoped would do the trick in the jungle. But we were all young and adventurous and resourceful enough, and we figured we'd make do with whatever circumstances presented themselves. We had food, we had water bottles, we had knives and matches, and we had a bottle of wine. What else did we need really? (Except perhaps a roll of duct tape?) Besides, if there was any truth to the whole Y2K hype, we were better off in the middle of the jungle than the middle of the city anyway.

We trekked on through the jungle for several hours, following the narrow but well-defined trail. Eventually it crossed over a pleasantly gurgling creek, and then came to a series of wide, stone steps that ascended a steep hill. At the bottom of the stone steps, we noticed a strange configuration of massive boulders jumbled together just off the trail.

We wandered over to investigate. To our surprise we discovered a partially hidden, roomy cave amidst the rocks, open on two sides, created by one huge boulder balanced on top of the others. We realized it was the perfect place to make camp for the night. There was a good seven or eight feet of headroom between the ground and the boulder balanced overhead, with a large, flat, open area, more than enough room to both make a fire and spread out our blankets on the dirt floor. There was plenty of ventilation for smoke from the fire to escape, and yet we would be protected in case it rained. We couldn't have asked for a better camping spot, or better timing. Evening was nearing and we were all tired, sweaty and getting on the verge of hungry. We unbuckled our backpacks, claimed our sleeping spots, and then set about collecting firewood before it got too dark.

As evening fell, we got the campfire blazing away in the center of the rock enclosure and started preparing dinner— vegetable stew and chapatis. We each pulled up a flat rock to sit on, as we chopped up vegetables and flattened out the chapati dough. We opened up the bottle of wine and started passing it around. The fire continued crackling away pleasantly, reflecting comforting light off the cave walls. The wine warmed our bellies.

Crickets and who-knew-what-else made shrill noises from the depths of the jungle. And, thanks to the Israeli chefs, the simmering stew emanated tantalizing smells worthy of any decent Indian restaurant.

Darkness descended, and our dinner was almost ready. We were perhaps two-thirds of the way through the bottle of wine, wholly relaxed, slightly giddy and looking forward to our homemade meal—the last one of the year, the decade, the century, the millennium.

Right about then, we heard strange voices in the nearby blackness, speaking unintelligibly, apparently in the local language. This caught us all off guard, since we had seen hardly anyone out there all day, and it was now pitch dark…not a good time for tourists to be wandering along down the trail through the jungle. Besides, we were all just buzzed enough to be slightly out of touch with reality, and certainly didn't want any distractions from either our good mood or our dinner. The disembodied voices got louder as they wandered in our direction, no doubt heading towards the light of our campfire. Finally two short, thin, unencumbered Indian men wandered into our cave and began speaking to us in an earnest tone, though still, of course, completely unintelligible to us.

We were at a total loss as to what to do. Although they didn't come across as hostile or even unfriendly, they clearly had something of import to convey to us. Fortunately Yossi knew a smidgen of Hindi (the predominant language of northern India, but not the local language of this area) and had learned a handful of words in the local tongue of Kannada. He tried his best to communicate in some fashion with them. Finally, Yossi thought he'd grasped a few familiar words, that made it apparent what it was they were trying to tell us: there were tigers in the surrounding jungle, and it wasn't safe to sleep there for the night. Perhaps, this cave was even one of the tigers preferred nighttime prowling spots.

Once we had determined that this was, indeed, the gist of what the two men had come to explain to us, we said thank you and "Namaste", and made it clear that we had understood their warning, and would heed it. They left our homely cave dwelling and continued on their way, their voices trailing off into the darkness of the jungle.

Yossi, Nadav and I all looked at each other in exasperation.

"Well, guys, so what do we do now?" I asked my Israeli friends.

"Fahking shit, man," said Yossi. "Look, our delicious food is almost done, we are enjoying our wine and now we have tigers coming to eat us. I don't know. What do you think, Nadav — what should we do? There is no more bus going back to town this evening, we have nowhere to sleep but in this crazy jungle."

We were all undoubtedly perplexed and annoyed.

"You know, I have an idea," said Nadav.

We listened attentively.

"I think that we should climb up on top of this big boulder over our heads, and eat our dinner up there."

"So, what about when it's time to sleep?" said Yossi.

"Well, we will sleep up there, too. We can carry everything to the top of the rock, and then no tigers can find us."

"Fahking tigers," said Yossi.

Since we had no idea if Nadav's plan was possible, we got off our half-drunk behinds and started looking around for ways to climb up the side of the massive boulder. Though it was a little tricky — especially in the dark and given our level of slight intoxication — eventually we did find what seemed like a feasible route up the rock, making use of the other boulders holding up the largest one. Nadav was eventually able to climb his way up, to stand triumphantly twenty or more feet above us. Then he yelled down:

"Yeah, man, it looks good! It's a little rough going up, you know, but it's mostly flat up here, and I think there is room for us to sleep."

"You think?" I yelled back.

"Yes, it is good. No problem—we will be quite comfortable. There are big grooves in the rock for sleeping, so no rolling off. And no tigers will be coming up here, even with our smelly stew. And, we will have the light of the stars over our heads."

With that, we started carrying our scattered belongings to the top of the boulder. We stuffed our backpacks and carried them to the top. Then we started bringing up the dirty pots and pans, chapatis and what was left of the bottle of wine. Lastly, we had to get our full pot of hot stew up there. I stood at the bottom of the rock and handed the pot up to Yossi, who then climbed partway and handed it off to Nadav at the top of the rock.

In a matter of fifteen or twenty minutes all of our things, including ourselves, were atop the enormous boulder that had previously been our ceiling. Though we no longer had our campfire, which we had put out, at least we now had the stars overhead to observe and ponder. We continued passing around the bottle of wine as we finally, hungrily, started in on the warm stew and chapatis.

"So, brother Gabriel," said Yossi, as he took a sip of wine. "You think the world is going to go crazy tonight? You believe all these things about the computers crashing from this bug, and disrupting our civilization, or something of this nature?"

"Man, you know, I really don't know what to think," I said. "It seems like just about anything could happen, from what I've heard. Maybe it will be just a blip, or maybe it will be total chaos. But I figure, humans survived for thousands of years before computers, and we'll survive through this one way or another, no matter what happens. It sounds like it could be a real mess. But shit, I don't know—maybe it's all just more media hype. Maybe they really did fix things. Or maybe it never was a problem in the first place, just a scheme for computer programmers to make a pile of money. Either way, I guess we'll be finding out for sure when we get back into town in a few days, eh?"

"Yeah, no shit," said Yossi. "I hope it messes things up a little, though. I think humanity needs a fahking wake-up call. Humans are fahking idiots."

"Yeah," I said. "I have to agree to some extent. Humans do need some serious waking up. Things have gotten way out of hand on this planet. We need to make a major change somehow, before it's too late. But if it doesn't come tonight, then I guess it'll probably come some other time. The natural order seems to prevail, one way or another. It's definitely a strange time we live in though, when people are afraid of a computer glitch bringing down Western civilization."

"No fahking shit," said Yossi.

A couple of hours later, the stew and wine long polished off, we were lying back on the rock on top of our blankets, watching the stars and enjoying our full bellies and a nice buzz. Nadav looked at his watch at one point, and announced to us:

"Guess what, my friends—it's midnight. It is now the year 2000. Welcome to the third millennium."

"Yeeee-ha," I said, lackadaisically.

"Shit, man—that's fahking crazy," said Yossi.

"Yeah," I agreed. "Weird. I wonder what's going on across the planet right now? It could be a completely different world that we're going back to—total anarchy and mayhem, modern civilization lying in ruins, the end of the world as we know it. How would we even know, way out here in the jungle?"

A couple of minutes later, a satellite arced slowly across the night sky. Its little red light blinked on and off, on and off as it cruised steadily along—same as they always do. I took that as an answer to my question, that the modern world was probably still humming along, much as usual. I wasn't really sure if I was happy or sad that the new millennium would likely be continuing just as the old one had ended. But at least I knew that I could still catch my return flight back home. I must admit, without modern technology, it would have been one hell of a long hitch.

Chapter 22

Always double-check the return policy (January 2000)

A few days after our harrowing New Year's Eve adventure, we emerged from the jungle unscathed, and reentered the relative normalcy of modern civilization at the dawning of the new millennium. I parted ways with Yossi and Nadav at that point, journeying south and then inland to the medium-sized city of Mysore, known for its exotic incense and perfumes. I planned to continue heading southwards to the very tip of India (or pretty darn close, at least) and then come back up through the eastern part of the country, heading north back towards Delhi as winter turned to spring and I neared my departure date in March.

It was a warm evening, the day after I'd rolled into town by bus from the coast. The sun had set and it was just beginning to get dark as I wandered somewhat aimlessly through the city streets. It was actually a welcome change to be in the frenzied activity of the city, after spending the past several weeks far from the pulsing crowds. The streets were filled with the usual bustle of Indians going about their routine business, the restaurants preparing for dinner customers, filling the air with the tantalizing scents of spiced vegetables, dahl, meat and curry dishes. I loved the intensity of the Indian people, and was glad to be back amidst the activity. There's so much happening in an Indian city at any given moment that it can be a fascinating adventure just to walk down the street—to see which animals will amble across your path, what sort of street acts might be taking place, who you'll end up conversing with (like it or not), what good deals you'll find, what religious shrines or ceremonies you should encounter.

I wasn't sure what I was doing with the rest of my evening, having just woken up from a late-afternoon nap back in my hotel room. I figured I'd probably just meander through the aromatic maze for a while, enjoying the sights and sounds of so many people going about their mundane, yet strange foreign lives. Eventually I'd likely find a small restaurant to hang out in, have a cheap thali for dinner and perhaps sip a chai.

I crossed a busy roundabout on my way to one of the main shopping streets, brushed off a few rickshaw taxi drivers looking for riders and continued walking towards another busy inter-section. As I was passing the local movie theater, plastered with brightly-colored posters portraying superficial romance, drama and action movies in unintelligible local script, an Indian *tout* (business hustler) came up alongside me—as they so often do, like a shadow hanging over your shoulder, acting like your best buddy.

"Hello, friend, you like to see good Indian music?" he asked.

"No thanks," I said firmly, giving him little of my attention. The problem is that if you say anything at all, or even glance their way, they take it as an encouraging sign. I admit that I wasn't the best at giving the cold shoulder, when perhaps it would have been in my best interest.

"Very nice, free music," he continued, urged on by my lack of complete disregard towards him. The Indian touts are quick to figure out which tourists can be pried into a conversation (and pried out of a rupee or two). "I'm going there right now, myself. I like to show tourists my city—no business. Very good, Indian sitar and tabla music, you will like."

Of course, "no business" is a deceptive half-truth, that means no business with them but rather with a friend of theirs who pays them commission to bring in business. The Indian businessmen are masters of the guilt trip. They can hook you if you're a vaguely friendly person, simply because they are so overly friendly themselves (oftentimes genuinely so, and others just plain manipulative).

One of the first tests of traveling in India is to get it through your head that you have no obligation to help the many strangers who will try and convince you otherwise, sad story or not. Learning to say no—and mean it—is essential if you don't want to be taken advantage of against your will, at almost every turn. This can undoubtedly be difficult when encountering mothers with hungry-looking children, cripples and sadhus (spiritual seekers) who depend on the handouts of others to survive. But if you tried to help everyone in India who approached you expecting assistance, you'd be in the same position after not too long. I'd gotten much better at handling these daily encounters over the past few months in India; though I was less gifted at the art of ignoring than some, who could walk along while a tout hounded them incessantly, without giving the slightest hint of acknowledgement.

But for a change, I actually decided to go along with him this time—just for the hell of it, to see what this guy was really about and perhaps even see some Indian music. I didn't have anything in particular to do right then and was in the mood for a little adventure. He seemed genuinely friendly and harmless, and I figured I'd just keep track of my whereabouts, then take off on my own whenever I got tired of his gig, whatever it might be. Maybe I would see some local sights that I otherwise wouldn't come across.

"Okay," I said. "Sure, take me to this music. What is your name?"

"Oh, very good sir, I am Patrul. Come with me, I show you very nice things along the way. Mysore is very fine city, you will see..."

I walked alongside him as we left the busy main street to head down a smaller side street, still active with the usual Indian bustle, but beginning to mellow with dusk.

"Beautiful city, Mysore, yes? This is my neighborhood," he

said, gesturing forward. "This is Muslim district, you see, this way. I am Hindu, but I have many Muslim friends."

"Oh, really," I said. "That's great, you live side-by-side pretty well here, do you?"

"Yes, in this city are all religions, Hindu, Muslim, Christian, Buddhist. Many Buddhists from Tibet are living near Mysore."

"Yes, that's right. I saw some of the Tibetan refugee camps on the way in on the bus."

"That's right, very friendly city, all people welcome— especially tourists! Many things to do here, very nice to visit."

Just then, he stopped abruptly at a tiny shrine sandwiched between the shops along the street. An altar was visible just inside, decorated with flower petals and half-burnt incense. "So, do you like to make *puja* now, sir?" (Puja is a spiritual prayer and offering that often involves giving money, especially when foreign tourists are involved.)

"Well, not really," I said honestly.

"Here—no charge—we make prayer, come inside with me."

He stepped into the small, sparsely decorated space and I followed behind, now that I had his word to hold him to. He stood at the altar in prayer for a few moments as I stood there in respectful silence. He then took a few rupees from his pocket and put them in a small bowl on the altar. We left and continued down the street. (I later wondered if this little show was designed to make him look religious, and thus trustworthy, in the case of any upcoming business dealings on our part.)

The sun had set by now and the evening light was fading into darkness. The street was lit now and again by low street lamps and shopkeepers' lights. I felt safe enough with this character, that he wasn't at all dangerous even if he did try to make a buck off me somehow. And besides, it was refreshing to talk with a local who knew a little more English than just "Which country?" and "Give me coin". He shared some of Mysore's history, including that of the local area.

"This is my neighborhood now," he said proudly. "Many Muslim, you see."

I agreed, noticing the apparent cultural shift, most noticeably in the many women shrouded in dark burqas.

"You like to see nice covered market?" Patrul then asked, as we crossed another street and neared a main thoroughfare. "Very nice market, you will like. Then I show you my brother's perfume shop." (Ah ha—so that was the deal.)

"Well, okay," I said. I was just going with the flow for the time being, getting a tour of the city beyond the thin tourist veil—and perfume was an integral part of this city's heritage. If I ended up walking away with a bottle of perfume, it wouldn't be such a bad thing.

We turned a corner and ducked under a small archway that led into an enclosed marketplace. It took up the entire center square of a city block, and was mostly hidden by the shops and other buildings lining the street. It had a low-hanging shade-cloth overhead, to keep out the sun during the sunny and warm winter days (and scorching summers no doubt). The floor was covered with scattered blankets spread out and piled with all sorts of produce. The sellers were either squatting before them patiently, or else going over their merchandise with customers. Because it was now late evening, things were clearly winding down. It was nice to see a smaller, more localized marketplace in India that wasn't quite so overcrowded and chaotic as the larger ones I'd been to. We wandered through as Patrul nodded hello to a few folks.

"You need anything, sir? Vegetables or rice for dinner?" Patrul asked me.

"No, thanks. I usually just eat out at restaurants. Very nice market though, it feels very local."

"Yes, mostly only people from this neighborhood are shopping here, few tourists coming...unless I bring them. Okay, now I show you my brother's perfume shop. You just take a look, no buy."

We left the marketplace through a different stone archway, that emptied us back out onto the street. We turned another corner, and after a half-block came to a handful of men talking in front of a shop. One of them looked up as we approached, and smiled.

"Ah, hello!" he said, addressing me in near-perfect English. "You have come to look at my shop?"

"Yeah, I guess so," I said. "I'm just looking around, you know—checking out the city for the evening."

"Okay, looking is fine, no pressure here, come inside please, sir."

He ushered me into his shop, along with Patrul and another man. The small room was filled with exotic, unnamable odors. He pulled up a couple of chairs, asked me to sit and then proceeded to open various small vials for me to smell, each with a more tantalizing aroma than the previous. He was clearly a savvy businessman, despite his projection of modesty, and I'm sure was hoping that I was an importer looking to make a big purchase. He told me that whatever I bought was guaranteed, and that he would refund my money if I wasn't fully satisfied. (Yeah right, like anyone ever got his or her money back in India.)

One of the perfumes he presented was apparently a natural mosquito repellent, which had a subtle but very pleasant smell. I decided to buy a small bottle, partly because I could use it since mosquitoes were often a nuisance in India, and also just to make a smooth exit, sans the guilt trip he seemed likely to give otherwise for the trouble of displaying his wares. Besides it was only 100 rupees, or about two dollars.

After paying, I said thanks and goodbye and then Patrul and I left the shop together. I was curious to see if he still planned to show me this Indian music, now that we'd done the business transaction.

"So, where is this music, Patrul?" I asked, ready to venture back to the more familiar part of town if he intended to take me to any more shops.

"This way, down this street, not far. It is festival tonight. Very good sitar music, you will like very much."

After several blocks, the street started to crowd with people. Sure enough, there seemed to be something celebratory going on. It continued to get more and more crammed and noisy as we made our way down the street. Whatever the event was, it seemed to be somewhere ahead of us. Soon the entire street was packed tight with smiling, boisterous Indians, most of them young men, staring at me unabashed and inquisitively as they passed by. Some of them made comments out loud, or else nodded hello with a boyish smirk. I was following just behind Patrul, doing my best to ignore the attention without being entirely unfriendly. The street was quickly turning into a dense sea of bodies. I was starting to think that I might rather be eating a meal alone in a quiet restaurant about now, than maneuvering through this congealing crowd.

"Hey, Patrul," I yelled to him above the noise. "How much further to this festival?"

"Oh, not far, soon we are there. No problem, you will like. Good Indian music, very nice." He seemed genuinely interested in showing me this musical event, so that I felt a little obliged to accept what felt like his heartfelt kindness.

"Alright," I said, a little more reluctantly. "But it better not be too far..."

The street was packed with bodies as far as I could see, and it was only getting more and more dense as we moved along. I was quickly tiring of the constant stares, giggles and comments in both Kannada (the local language) and occasional English phrases (such as the ever-witty "Hello, English!").

As we continued moving (or rather, being moved) slowly along, my interest in catching the musical event was rapidly dwindling, when I felt a hand momentarily on my back pocket from someone going by. I looked back, but of course couldn't tell who had done it amidst the throng. Fortunately, I didn't carry anything in my pockets. But that pretty well made up my mind.

"Hey, Patrul," I yelled. "I'm going. Too many people."

"You leave? No see music?"

"No, thank you, it's too crowded. How do I get back from here?"

"Okay, no problem, I get you taxi."

At the next intersection he walked up to an auto rickshaw, spoke to the driver briefly in Kannada, ushered me into the back seat and waved goodbye. Finally I was on my way, glad to be leaving behind the intensity of the crowd. I had little idea of where in the city I was at that point. But there's never a shortage of rickshaw or taxi drivers in India, who can always take you back to the main tourist center for a relative pittance, no matter where you might end up in your wanderings.

After winding for fifteen or twenty minutes through unfamiliar territory, I began to recognize things as we neared my hotel. The taxi driver then dropped me off at the same large roundabout where I'd originally met Patrul. After paying him ten rupees, or twenty-five cents, I continued walking along down the same street where I'd been an hour or two earlier.

I came to another busy intersection after a few blocks. My stomach was noisily rumbling away by now. I stood at the inter-section momentarily, considering which of two enticingly odorous restaurants to frequent for dinner—when a short, wrinkled old Indian woman walked up to me and said, in a splitting English accent:

"Now, how can I help you, young man? You look a tad perplexed."

I was altogether taken aback by her clear speech and perfect accent. Although many Indians spoke some degree of English, they were most often shopkeepers or businessmen, and generally had the thick, cliché, lilting Indian accent that the average

American would recognize portrayed on TV shows, often involving convenience stores. But now, it was as if there was a proper, upstanding English lady standing before me, somehow speaking out of this short little old Indian woman.

"Oh, well thanks," I said. "I'm not lost, actually. I'm just trying to make up my mind which of these restaurants to go to for dinner."

"Well, there's a great little restaurant right across the street over there that I highly recommend. Would you care to join me? I haven't eaten myself, and I'd love to have the chance to converse with you. It's not terribly often that I get to speak at length in English with a Westerner."

I had actually been looking forward to a quiet meal alone, after the previous dramatic events. But of course, it was hard to turn her down. And besides, the theme of the evening seemed to be to just go along for the ride, and see what strangeness might transpire next.

"Sure," I said. "What sort of restaurant is it? I'm in the mood for a *masala dosa*." (A thin pancake filled with spicy potatoes, and coconut sauce on the side.)

"Oh, I'm sure they have that," she said. "It's your standard Indian fare."

We strolled across the street, entered the restaurant and sat down at a small table. We both ordered. Then she asked me the usual inquisitive questions, such as where I was from, what I was doing in India, whether I was married, what I did for a living. She also shared a bit of her own story. It turned out she had a Master's degree from Cambridge (thus the impeccable English accent) and was a collector of foreign oddities—and wondered if I might have something from the United States that I'd care to donate to her collection. Apparently there were contests among local collectors to see who could acquire the most unique items from different countries. She had, so she stated proudly, won first prize three years in a row. She was a little disappointed to hear that I had nothing I could give her. But I had nothing with me that I didn't need, and besides most of my traveling possessions were from India by now.

Somewhere in the course of our conversation, I happened to mention the mosquito repellent perfume I'd just bought.

"Where did you buy it?" she asked.

"Just one of these touts that came up to me. He took me to his brother's shop up a side street."

"Was it a Hindu perfume shop in the Muslim district, near a produce market?"

"Well, yes, actually."

"Oh dear, I know those men — and they are complete frauds. What sort of perfume did you buy?"

I took the little bottle out of my pocket, unscrewed the top and handed it to her. She smelled it. "Hmmm, Tiger Lily. How much did you pay for it?"

"A hundred rupees. He said it keeps away mosquitoes. It seems like he called it something else, though."

"Well, he ripped you off, young man," she said resolutely. "This doesn't repel mosquitoes at all. In fact, it attracts them. I know what perfume he was talking about, and that would have been a fair price for the real thing. But it's much more expensive to make, so he gave you this cheap generic stuff. That man always takes advantage of the tourists. There is another shop two doors down from that one, which is reputable. I want you to go back to this man, and get very irate, and tell him you want your money back and that you're going to tell all the foreigners he's a crook and not to buy from him. He needs to learn his lesson."

"Oh, okay," I said. Though I was a little irked at this news, I wasn't quite that irate over paying two dollars for some perfume. It still smelled nice. "Well, maybe I'll go talk to him tomorrow. He did say he would refund my money if I wanted."

"Yes, you must go back to him and get very angry, speak very loud and firm and tell him that you're going to spread the word about him and ruin his business if he doesn't shape up. They are not bad men, but they *are* bad businessmen..."

After dinner, and a pleasant rest of the conversation (except for the part where she presumed that I was paying the bill, even though *she* had invited *me*—but again, it was hard to turn her down), I said goodbye and thanks for the pertinent information, and started walking back towards my hotel. On the way there I passed by another marketplace that I'd wandered through a few days earlier. I remembered that I'd seen another perfume seller there. I decided to stop in and see if he could confirm what sort of perfume I'd bought. Although many of the shops were closing up for the night and there were few customers around, I was able to find the shop. The old man who owned it was still there, just starting to close things up.

"Namaste," I said, and then held up the small bottle of perfume. "Can you tell me what kind is this?"

He didn't speak much English. "What kind? Oh, okay—I see?"

I handed him the bottle, he unscrewed the cap and sniffed. "This Tiger Lily," he said assuredly, confirming what the elderly lady had told me.

"You have the kind for mosquitoes?" I asked.

"Mosquitoes? Ah, yes..."

He grabbed a bottle from the counter in front of him, unscrewed it and handed it to me. I sniffed. It smelled much more like something to keep away mosquitoes—still an agreeable odor, but more pungent and distinct than the subtle Tiger Lily perfume I had unknowingly bought.

"Okay, I'll take this bottle."

"One-hundred rupees," he said with a smile, clearly pleased to have made a last-minute sale.

I walked back towards my hotel, figuring to get my money back for the fake stuff the next day. I was starting to get a little more annoyed about the bad deal, the more I thought about it. As

I was about to walk up the steps to the hotel, I decided that I wanted to get it over with right then, while the deal was still fresh in the perfume-seller's memory. I had a rental bike locked in front of the hotel. I thought I could find the perfume shop okay on my own, since it was basically straight up from the roundabout where I'd met the tout, and there was the distinctive arched entranceway to the nearby market.

I unlocked the bike and rode quickly in the direction of the shop, working up my courage to confront the owner. He seemed the type that made a strong show of himself as being reasonable and reputable, and I suspected that his pride wouldn't allow him to go back on his word face-to-face.

I came to the market entrance, hung a right turn and soon came to the shop. The same group of men was still standing there, laughing and talking loudly into the night. The shop owner gave a fake half-smile, as I pulled up abruptly on my bike, clearly not happy to see me given my hasty and assertive demeanor. I didn't plan to make a scene—I just wanted my money back.

"This isn't the kind of perfume you said it was," I said right away. "I took it to another shop. I want my money back."

"Oh, no, that is the real perfume. Which shop? He was probably lying," he said. He clearly didn't want to be embarrassed by a foreigner in front of his associates.

"Look, you said you would give me my money back—I want my money back."

He muttered to himself, then reached into his pocket with a bit of a grimace, pulled out a large roll of money, found a 100 rupee note and handed it to me. I handed him back the bottle.

"Thanks," I said, for some reason.

With that I biked off and headed back towards my hotel room—glad I'd stood up to him, even if I didn't make a big scene like the old Indian woman had said. The 100 rupees wasn't enough to get that excited about, though in India I could buy a couple of complete meals, or a new cotton shirt with it. But it seemed more important to make something of an impression on yet another petty Indian crook, who wasn't desperate for the money (given the large wad of bills he'd pulled out of his pocket).

Not that it would make much difference. He would doubtless continue to rip off tourists, as long as it put more cash in his pocket. At least in this case it was just a bottle of perfume—not such a big deal. I had been in the mood for some adventure, and I'd found it. Next time I'd just say "No, thanks" as usual and keep on walking, knowing full well what these touts were all about. But at least I did get my money back for once. And yes the other stuff did, in fact, keep away the mosquitoes...somewhat.

Chapter 23

Don't fool around with the locals' women
(February 2000)

The erotic tourist attraction known as Khajuraho is one of the most impressive physical manifestations of tantric spirituality in India, perhaps in the world. Its construction is for the most part lost to history. In the center of India, in the middle of nowhere, are scattered dozens of extraordinary temples dedicated solely to the art of lovemaking. The outside walls of the temples—some as high as a hundred feet—are completely covered with intricate stone carvings of humans (and non-humans) molded and twisted into every conceivable sexual position. If these carvings had been representations of people in prayer, it would have been a marvel of religious worship and craftsmanship. As detailed depictions of the human sexual act, it was a mystery of profound curiosity and titillation.

The temples of Khajuraho are located in the vicinity of what used to be the capital of an empire, but is now a small but thriving tourist town of the same name. I stayed there for three days, in a cheap but pleasant hotel in town of the usual Indian variety—thin, hard mattress, squat toilet, the occasional scurrying cockroach, an accessible rooftop for basking in the ever-present sunshine—for the equivalent of a dollar-fifty a night. For a few dollars more I could have stayed in a midrange hotel, but as usual I was on a budget, even by Indian standards.

The one problem with this tourist area (other than simply being touristy) was that the ever-present shopkeepers were so overwhelmingly sociable; it was hard to get around the village without a persistent hassle. Most of them were young, hip, enthusiastic businessmen catering to the prevalent European package tourists. But because the town was small and so far from anything, they seemed starved for some stimulating social interaction other than sitting around all day selling trinkets to kinky tourists—such as talking with the few younger adventure travelers who came through town.

Walking down the street, I encountered a constant barrage of offers for chai and conversation. But I didn't drink chai much, due to the concentrated caffeine—especially in the middle of a hot day—and I wasn't that into repeated conversations with Indian shopkeepers. They tended to ask all the same questions with their limited English, and eventually, of course, lead to urgings to look around and buy something. Besides, I wasn't there to hang out in the dusty town and look at souvenirs, but to check out the temples in the outlying area. I found that renting a bicycle managed to solve most of the problem. Cruising quickly down the street, there wasn't enough time for them to get in more than a "Namaste" as I coasted quickly by.

Quandary resolved, I spent the first day just biking around and visiting the ornate temples. They were truly astounding. I could hardly conceive of the thousands of hours of painstaking work that must have been involved in creating such detailed images from pure stone. The figures were carved deep into the thick walls of the stone temples, covering virtually every square foot of the temple's exteriors. Each individual carving was a few feet in diameter, with other carvings directly on every side. It seemed that each separate carving must have taken weeks or months to create. And yet, there were hundreds and hundreds of them covering the outside walls of almost two-dozen temples—almost every single image a depiction of the sexual act in myriad forms. And it was believed that there had been many more of these temples, most of which had been lost to wars and other ravages of time.

What sort of cultural paradigm had previously existed here to create this? This was a commonly asked question, which apparently would go unanswered, since little was known about the people and culture of those who had lived on these plains during the several-hundred years in which the structures were believed to have been built. There was nothing quite like it anywhere else in India. Though there were common sexual references in Indian art and Hindu spiritual depictions—as well as their explicit book of love, the *Kama Sutra*—nowhere else in India were there ornate temples devoted solely to the art of sex. It was apparently a long lost religion. Too bad.

The following day, talking with the owners of my hotel about other things to do in the area, they informed me of a waterfall outside of town which they recommended as a good destination for a bicycle ride. They said it was about ten or fifteen miles by road and then a short hike up a path to the waterfall. With their tentative directions in mind, I decided to check it out. If I didn't find the waterfall, then at least I'd see some more of the countryside and get a little exercise and fresh air in the process.

I headed down the road out of town on my rental bike, cruising along comfortably through the dry Indian countryside, enjoying the feeling of the wind rushing through my hair. The Indian rental bikes seemed modeled after those from 1950s America—heavy cruisers with a large, bouncy triangular seat, fat tires and wide handlebars, so that you could really kick back and relax as you pedaled along.

Following the simple directions, after a mile or so I turned right onto a smaller road that headed across a wide valley, towards some gentle hills. Simple huts were scattered alongside the road, some accompanied by green farmer's fields in contrast to the surrounding dry grasslands. Indian farmers, men and women, young and old were busy working in many of them. They would often look up at me as I rode by, sometimes even waving and shouting hello.

As I passed by one of these fields, I heard a shout from a woman working at the far end of the field, which seemed directed at me. I turned around and pedaled back out of curiosity—to see the woman running through the field towards me. I stopped and waited on my bike, as she crossed the field, climbed over a low fence and then came up onto the road.

"Namaste," I said.

"Namaste," she replied, a little breathless.

Now, I can't really say that we carried on a conversation, since my Hindi was paltry and she clearly didn't know a word of English. But we managed to carry on a fairly awkward yet engaging interaction of some kind for a good ten or so minutes. She was fairly young—hard to say but maybe early twenties— and beautiful, as so many of the Indian women are, with dark skin, long dark hair, deep brown eyes, long earrings and of course wearing an elegant, colorful sari.

Considering that I'd just spent the previous day viewing erotic temple art, this beautiful young Indian woman running up to me from a farmer's field seemed like a natural prelude to something more, well, erotic. Continuing the obvious story-line from here (at least in my imagination), wasn't I now supposed to toss my bike into a nearby bush and then she'd lead me into the nearby tall grass where I would remove her clothing to reveal her taut, darkened skin, and then revel in her exquisite nakedness as she whispered poetry to me in her native tongue? Or at least something along those lines?

But for all I knew, she was married and her husband was one of the people working alongside her. Not a recommended traveler's habit, to go around stealing the locals' women from under their noses, even if for just an afternoon or two. And besides, I wasn't trapped in a romance novel as I may have wished, but in very real India. Chances are she just wanted a rupee—and probably found me unappealing anyway, with my pale skin and blond hair.

But if I *were* writing my own romance novel, then I would have had the village genie transform me into her young male suitor, just for a day or so. And then we would break all the local taboos by romping unabashedly in the tall grass. Although considering the nearby temples, perhaps we wouldn't even have to break any taboos. We would just be worshipping, following the divine example carved so carefully into stone. Come on, where was a good genie when you needed one?

But until such an implausible fantasy presented itself, I would have to soak up the young woman's enigmatic beauty while it paused fleetingly in front of me, and be satisfied with the momentary captivation. Until my fiction became non, the tall grass would still be there, or at least somewhere.

The woman had with her a handful of green beans, obviously whatever she was harvesting in the field; which she offered to me, as I said "Namaste" a few more times and "*Ach-cha, ach-cha*" (good/okay). I took the green beans and munched on one. I soon noticed three other people coming across the field, who also climbed over the fence and came up to the road to join us. One was a young boy, the other a young girl (perhaps siblings), and the third an older woman who could have been her mother.

I searched through my daypack to see what I could give them in return for the green beans, and came up with a few pieces of Indian mango candy. I offered them each a piece, and they took it enthusiastically, popping it into their mouths and then standing there sucking and staring at me. I also offered them a drink from my water bottle, and they all drank from it eagerly. Perhaps they were hoping I might purchase some of their fresh vegetables. Or maybe they just wanted to see a foreigner up close and personal. I'll never know, because eventually they simply wandered back out to the field to continue their work. And I continued biking down the road.

After riding along for another hour or so, I came to a little pay station beside the road, with one of those wooden arms for halting cars reaching halfway across the road. Four Indian men were sitting back in plastic chairs nearby, in the ample shade of a line of trees. Apparently the waterfall I was looking for was within a park of some kind (not mentioned by my hotel owners), and this was a pay point for cars entering the park. I biked casually past the line of men lazing beneath the trees, intending to go around the wooden rail, in the usual budget traveler's mode of when-in-doubt-assume-you-don't-have-to-pay-unless-someone-tells-you-to (hoping that bicycles were exempt) when one of them whistled at me. I turned around, and biked back to the men.

"One-hundred rupees," said one of the men to me, who didn't look very official at all—just a guy sitting on the side of the road.

"Ha, ha," I said, thinking he was pulling my leg, just trying to make an easy buck off a dumb tourist. A hundred rupees was altogether unreasonable, for what seemed a very ordinary park in the middle of nowhere. The vast zoo back in Mysore had been only eight rupees. The world famous Taj Mahal had been fifteen (though just a few months after I'd visited, they jacked it up to 800).

"See the sign?" he said, pointing at the shack.

I pedaled over to the shack. Sure enough, there was a sign: Entrance fee—RS 5 per car. Tourist price—RS 100 per car. (Tourist meaning non-Indian.)

"Damn," I said. "Even if I'm on a bike?" I asked.

"One-hundred rupees," he said, with an almost-imperceptible grin.

I wasn't about to blow 100 rupees just for a waterfall, whether or not it was the actual fee. That was more than the price of my hotel room. I'd seen enough waterfalls in my life for free. Instead, I decided just to take a break there in the shade, and then head back to town. I noticed that a couple of the men were sucking on soda bottles.

"Where do you get a soda around here?" I asked.

"Store down the road," the same man pointed, just inside the park.

I looked down the road past the pay station, and could see a small shack off the road, through the trees.

"Okay if I go, if I leave my bike?" I asked, gesturing in that direction.

"Okay," he said. These guys seemed hard to rile. I probably could have just kept biking past them, and it would have been way too much trouble for them to get up and go after me.

But I left the bike by the road, then wandered down to the little store, bought a soda and walked back to my bike and the bored fee collectors. There was a vacant plastic chair nearby, that one of the men pointed me at. I sat down in the shade and joined the club, as I sucked away on my own soda. After some more similarly in-depth conversation, and eventually draining my soda, I stuffed the empty bottle into my daypack, hopped on my bike, waved goodbye—four waves back amidst slurping—and then pedaled my way back towards town.

Chapter 24

Immersed in the crowd
(February 2000)

From Khajuraho I bused north, heading towards the bustling cities of Allahabad and Varanasi, along the sacred Ganges River. I wanted to visit Allahabad purely because of the Magh Mela ceremony. Otherwise it was just another congested, noisy and industrious Indian city.

The Magh Mela is a smaller version of the massive Hindu spiritual gathering known as the Kumbha Mela. The Kumbha Mela is in the Guinness Book of World Records for being the largest human gathering ever known to take place. The 1969 Woodstock Festival at half a million people pales in comparison, with the Kumbha Mela attracting somewhere between 15 and 30 million — or around two or three times the entire population of New York City. It might help the imagination to know that India is the second most populous country in the world and now contains well over a billion people, or more than 15% of the entire world's population. In other words, if you should happen to reincarnate, you have about a one in six chance of finding yourself an Indian.

The Magh Mela, though much smaller than the Kumbha Mela, is still significant for those who attend. The Kumbha Mela occurs every four years in one of four different holy Indian cities. The smaller Magh Mela takes place the interspersing three years, for the more committed Hindu devotees. My travel guide had given a fair amount of information on the Kumbha Mela, and briefly mentioned that the Magh Mela would be happening in late February of 2000, in Allahabad. I'd been making a beeline the past few weeks from southern India to Varanasi — one of the holiest and most-visited Indian cities along the Ganges River—and decided to stop through Allahabad on my way there, to hopefully catch a glimpse of this unique and significant spiritual event. In a way, it sounded like an Indian version of a Rainbow Gathering.

I arrived in Allahabad, got off the bus and was immediately accosted by a half dozen bicycle rickshaw drivers. I picked one randomly and asked him to take me to a cheap hotel. But we had a hard time finding a vacant room, I guessed because of the Magh Mela ceremony. Finally we found a hotel with an available room. It was a little more expensive than I preferred at 300 rupees (seven dollars). But it was also one of the nicer rooms I'd had in a while, with nice carpeting, a wide bed, decent mattress (better than most at least) and even a TV. It was worth spending the money to stay somewhere altogether pleasant for a change, as well as to get a little taste of Indian television (bizarre, to say the least).

After checking in and then being shown to the room, I was in the process of unpacking while watching some Indian music videos on the TV, when I heard a knock at the door. I opened it, to the same bellboy who had just shown me to my room a few minutes earlier.

"Yes?" I said.

"Sir, there is a friend here to see you," he said.

Puzzled, I was about to explain to him that he must have the wrong room, since no one I knew on the planet was aware that I was in Allahabad. But then a large man, late thirties, dark purple beret at a rakish angle covering his thick, curly red hair, and a big grin, stepped into view.

"Hey, you must be Gabriel," he said, offering his hand. "I'm Stan. I saw your name in the register downstairs and noticed that you were from Ukiah, California. I'm from Berkeley."

My consternation quickly turned to exuberance. "Wow, hey, nice to meet you Stan," I said, shaking his hand vigorously. "No shit! Berkeley, eh? I actually graduated from Berkeley High School."

"Really?" he said, looking as surprised as myself now. "Me, too! That's amazing. What year did you graduate?"

"1989."

"Yeah, I graduated a decade earlier, '79. That's crazy. Seriously small world."

"Definitely," I said. "I wasn't expecting to meet many foreigners in Allahabad of all places, especially from so close to home...So how goes the travels?"

"Pretty good, pretty good. Just flew in a couple of days ago actually, came straight here. Great to finally be in India again. So, you in town for the Magh Mela? That's all I'm here for, just making a short trip this time."

"Well, yeah," I said, hoping he might have some more current information, since my travel guide was about six years old. "I am, but I don't know much of anything about it—like when or where it's happening, for example. I assume you must know a little more than that."

"Yeah, man, you're right on time—tomorrow's the big day," he said. "A million people are expected to be there."

"No way, that's awesome..." I said, grateful for my fortunate timing. I hadn't been sure if I was within a week, let alone a day. The date wasn't announced with certainty beforehand, because it depended on the determination of Indian astrologers who conferred on the best date, as it got closer to the event. "That's great to hear, I'm really looking forward to the experience. I had no idea it would be that large of a gathering. My guidebook said maybe a few hundred-thousand, but it's outdated by six years, so I really didn't know what to expect."

He then invited me over to his room, where he was staying with two other travelers—another guy from the States and a fellow from Germany. After unpacking, I wandered over to their room and hung out for a while, happy to have some company to tell my recent traveling tales. I also got some basic directions from them to the location of the Magh Mela, though he said that any rickshaw driver would be able to take me right there, as it was undoubtedly the big event in town. As the evening turned late, I said goodbye to the three travelers and perhaps I would see them the next day amidst the crowds, since us Western folks do tend to stand out.

What can I possibly say to convey such numbers? Imagine masses upon masses upon masses of people, farther than one could see. According to a local newspaper article, it drew more than one-and-a-half-million Hindu pilgrims—far more than previous years, for some reason. I'd decided to stretch my legs and walk to the gathering site the next morning, following Stan's basic directions—take a right from the hotel down the main street, turn left at the next major intersection and then follow the crowd for another mile or so, keeping an eye open for the Ganges River and the teeming multitudes. Hard to miss.

As I neared the apparent site, the Ganges not yet visible, the crowd along the street steadily thickened. Eventually I came to a congested intersection, where people were coming from all directions and funneling into a large clearing by the road. At that point I was engulfed by the huge crowd and went with its sluggish flow, the masses ever-increasing in size and density as we moved steadily along through an open field. Eventually we came to a wide, dusty path, heading towards the main gathering area along the river. The crowd was like a river itself now, with other streams and creeks of people flowing into it as we headed down the path of least resistance.

The wide path led up a small hill. Coming over the crest of the hill, we came into view of another huge clearing, filled with large, white canvas tents. The crowd ahead flowed down the hill and then spread among the white tents like water rushing over boulders, filling all possible spaces in between. I moved with the massive crowd down the hill, and then along the main path that continued through the swarm of tents and people, which then led to another hill, sloping downwards.

At the top of that hill, I was greeted with the awesome sight of the sacred Ganges. Although I had seen it and even swam in it before, farther upstream at Rishikesh where it was just leaving the mountains, it was a much different river here: wider, slower, dirtier and also seemingly wiser and more experienced. Before, I'd witnessed the exuberant, fresh and clear 20-year-old Ganges. This was the same river 30 years later, with a heavy weight on its back, and many stories to tell.

The constantly swelling crowd continued flowing down to the river's edge. At the bottom of this hill the path and the masses met the river's edge. The river was a few hundred yards wide—a murky, thick, relentless mass of dark brown, muddy, polluted water forging along like a team of slow-moving oxen, with little apparent care for whomever might fall in and be carried along by its mighty force. Saddling the river was a narrow, floating pontoon bridge, which was full to capacity with people crossing to the other side. On the far side of the river was another large area speckled with more white tents and seemingly endless throngs of Hindu devotees. About 100 yards further down the river another pontoon bridge crossed the river, also filled to capacity with throngs of people shuffling along. I soon realized that the two bridges were each one-way, in opposing directions over the river. The dense flow of the crowd made it so there was no possibility of crossing in the opposite direction on the same bridge. To come back across the river, you would have to make your way down along the bank to the other bridge and then cross there.

I continued being taken along by the crowd down to the river. After waiting for a while for the crowd ahead to funnel onto the bridge, I stepped onto the bridge myself. It was about five feet wide, with large barrels acting as flotation devices which were jerking from side to side with the force of the river rushing below. A thick cable guardrail ran the length of both sides. Once stepping onto the bridge, I was moved along with little volition of my own, as if on an escalator, until I was deposited finally on the other side.

I spent the next few hours just wandering around amongst the masses of people, in humbled awe. I never saw Stan and friends, or any other foreign travelers for that matter. Hundreds of thousands of Indian men, women and children were gathered along the wide bank of the muddy river—bathing, meditating, talking, laughing, praying, immersing sacred objects into the river, dipping their hands in and then bringing the water to their mouths to drink. I removed my shoes and walked among the devotees, dipping my feet briefly into the cold, murky water. Then I sat down on a hill a little ways from the river, to just sit and observe the momentous spiritual spectacle for a while.

Chapter 25

The end of a journey
(March 2000)

As spring approached, I continued traveling north. My flight was leaving mid-March and I wanted to at least get a glimpse of the Himalayan mountain range before flying back home. I journeyed by train from Varanasi on the Ganges, to the foothills of the snow-covered Himalaya, east of where I'd been over four months earlier in the Himalayan foothills at Rishikesh. I then took a bus further up into the mountains. I stayed for five days at a guesthouse near the small mountain village of Almora, perched on a narrow ridge overlooking a wide valley, from which I had a clear view of the endless towering peaks of the snowy Himalaya forty or fifty miles away.

I spent plenty of time in my five days there just hanging out and gazing in wonder at the snow-covered peaks, which were some of the highest in the Himalaya. This region of the world was a place of such legend—of both Western triumph and tragedy, and of Eastern mysticism and miracles. The Himalayan Mountains encapsulated such primal, natural energy, at the same time cradling deep history of human culture and spirituality. They seemed to capture the full intensity of both life and death. Much like that mountain range in Alaska as we drove along down the highway, I could sense their life-giving vitality pouring out from them, spreading to other lands and people far away. The difference here, of course, was that a whole nation, Tibet, actually occupied these mountains, rather than only animals and trees. The border was just on the other side of the peaks I was gazing at. It seemed somehow as if peering out at them, I were looking simultaneously through a window into the distant past of humanity, that filled my imagination with endless visions and ponderings of those who had lived there, died there and escaped persecution by braving those mountains in order to escape to India. The Dalai Lama, spiritual leader of Tibet, still lived in India after decades of exile, at Dharamsala a ways northwest, in a different part of the Indian Himalaya.

From Almora I took a harrowing series of bus rides that skirted those very mountains I'd been viewing from my guesthouse; and which eventually brought me back down to the spiritual village of Rishikesh along the Ganges River, straddling the Himalayan foothills and the vast Ganges plains. It was reinvigorating to see familiar territory in India. Being there brought back all the sights, sounds and smells of my introduction to this crazy, beautiful country; and reminded me of just how much I'd seen and experienced in the past five months. This time I only stayed there a couple of days, in a simple room at one of the many ashrams in the area alongside the Ganges. My flight left Delhi in just a few short days.

Leaving Rishikesh, I took a bus south to Haridwar, also along the Ganges. From there I would hop on a train to Delhi. I made a train reservation at the ticket counter early that afternoon, and stored my backpack at the luggage counter. The next train didn't leave until ten o'clock that night, arriving in Delhi early the next morning, so I had plenty of time to kill.

I had passed briefly through Haridwar on my way to Rishikesh at the beginning of my trip, but hadn't spent any time there. It was one of the four holy cities that hosted the Kumbha Mela every four years, though the town itself was much smaller than Allahabad. They held a daily spiritual prayer ceremony by the Ganges every evening, called an *aarti* ceremony. I figured I would wander around town for the afternoon, and then catch the ceremony at sundown.

I walked from the train station up the main street in the direction of the Ganges. When I eventually arrived at the ceremonial site by the river, it was around four in the afternoon. I still had a couple hours before the evening event, and not much in mind to do until then. I checked out a small souvenir shop, bought a t-shirt, and then decided to do a little random exploring. I walked across a bridge over the Ganges, which led to a small footpath going away from town.

As I wandered away from the river, I passed a few locals on the path. Eventually I came to a typical Indian shantytown. Though I had seen plenty of these ramshackle communities from buses and trains, I'd never really seen one up close. A small tributary of the Ganges was flowing nearby—and apparently the gravel riverbed near the water was the community toilet. In summer, when the monsoon rains came, the waste would all be flushed down the river. Until then, it would sit on the rocks in little piles and attract flies.

A flimsy arrangement of structures was perched on the riverbank, made from plastic, cardboard and tin. Children played together in the sand on the riverbank, and men and women went about their business among the makeshift housing. I walked along the edge of the gravel riverbed just below the village, until I came to a woman washing her laundry in the water, who looked up at me with some apparent surprise. I nodded "Namaste" and kept walking, as she nodded and then went back to her work.

There were some strategically placed stones sticking out of the shallow river water, leading across the small tributary to another path on the other side. I crossed the river, jumping from stone to stone, and then continued walking up the path. It wound through some dense brush and tall dry grass. After walking for a little ways without reaching anything interesting, I turned around and walked back to the river.

When I came back to the riverbank at the crossing point, there were two young boys huddled over something on one of the stones in the middle of the water. I realized that it was a very large, dead snake—possibly a cobra, though I couldn't be sure. They left the snake lying on one of the stones, then ran up towards me on the riverbank to hide behind a bush and watch the reaction of the next person crossing the river. I decided to take a seat and watch the local entertainment.

Eventually an older man came along, and hopped from one stone to the next across the shallow river. Just as he was about to hop onto the rock where the dead snake lay, he saw it, and suddenly hopped into the water. Fortunately it was hardly knee-deep. Once he'd gotten over his fright, he ventured a little closer to the snake and realized that it was dead. He then grabbed it by the tail, waded the rest of the way across the river, and threw the snake into a bush at the water's edge. As he walked up the riverbank he saw me sitting there and gave a look of "So—you're the prankster?" I just shrugged and he continued walking up the path.

Meanwhile, the two young boys were giggling away in the bushes. Once the old man was gone, they came out of their hiding place and went to the bush to fetch the dead snake. They took it back to the river, and again laid it on one of the rocks. Then they came up onto the riverbank, this time sitting down near me. One of the boys looked over at me, pointed towards the dead snake and chuckled. I chuckled back.

We sat there for a few more minutes, awaiting the next victim. Soon enough a woman came walking down the riverbed on the far side and started across the river using the rocks. Just as she was about to hop onto the rock with the snake, she stopped and gasped—almost jumping into the water, but not quite. She hunched forward to look closer. Then she looked up at the three of us sitting there on the riverbank, the two boys giggling away, and gave a little chuckle herself. She hopped onto the rock next to the snake, picked it up and examined it for a minute, then tossed it into the river. The two boys gave a cry of protest. But it was already floating away. They would just have to find another game to entertain themselves for the day.

I decided to head back into town and do a little more perusing of the shops. I hopped back over the river, walked up the gravel riverbank and took the path leading to the bridge over the main part of the Ganges and into town. I had at least another hour before the evening ceremony. I walked up one of the main streets lined with countless shops and restaurants, to watch the people and look over the wide assortment of goods for sale, and perhaps get a few more souvenirs.

After walking for a while, I eventually neared what seemed to be the other end of town. I turned around and started back. Evening was finally approaching, and the ceremony would be taking place right after sundown. I crossed the street for a change of scene, and then picked up my pace a little, since I had wandered a good ways from the river in the course of my walk.

At one point I happened to turn around and look back down the street from where I'd just come. I was intrigued to see a long line of old, colorfully painted Indian buses coming slowly down the street towards me. My first thought was that it was strange to see buses actually going slowly in India, since usually the driver practically had his elbow on the horn, scaring people and animals out of the way just as they're about to be run over. And also it was odd to see them lined up behind one another like some sort of procession. They were still a ways off, and the line disappeared around a curve so that I couldn't tell how many buses there were.

A little while later I looked back again—and though the line of buses was beginning to near me, I still couldn't see the end of it. As the buses came closer, I could see that they were all filled beyond capacity, much more so than even the usual passenger buses—people were packed tightly inside, hanging out of the doors and windows and seated casually on the luggage racks on top. It appeared to be a caravan of some kind, as if an entire village were on the move. I could see dozens of buses by now.

But they still continued coming into view, one at a time, from around the bend down the road.

I continued walking along, as the line of buses neared me and then slowly began to pass. They obviously meant to stick close together, as they were moving barely faster than my brisk walk. But by the relaxed looks on the people's faces, they weren't in a terrible hurry to get wherever they were headed. I noticed that all of the men were wearing turbans; so concluded that they must be Sikhs rather than Hindus. Perhaps they were on a pilgrimage of some sort. I saw that many of the Indians on the street were stopping what they were doing to watch the caravan go by; and realized this wasn't a common occurrence even for the locals. The unusual energy of the caravan and the thousands of people who were a part of it seemed to take over the town. For a change, I wasn't the object of curiosity. The men, women and children stared out of the packed buses and from atop the luggage racks, as the people of the village and myself stared back at them from the street.

A couple of young men yelled down at me from atop one of the passing buses.

"Hello, English, how are you?"

I looked up, and they waved at me. I smiled and waved back—and then they gestured at me, to hop on the bus and come up on top to join them.

"Come up there?" I said back to them.

"Yes," one of the young men yelled down to me. "Come up, we can give you ride through town, since you are walking."

I thought about it for a moment, but then yelled up to them, "Thank you, I'm not going that much farther—I like walking for now."

"Okay," he said. "Have good day!"

I smiled and continued walking as they ever so slowly passed me. I suppose that could have been my chance to catch a ride, and be able to say I'd hitchhiked in India—another country to add to the list. But for some reason, I just wanted to be an observer. I was content just walking alongside this extraordinary cultural phenomenon, observing the radiant, peaceful masses of people packed into dozens of old, creaky Indian buses as they stared back at me, just as curious.

It occurred to me to at least ask the young men where they were headed, while I had the chance.

So I yelled up to them, "Where are all these buses going?"

"We are Sikhs," the young man yelled down to me. "We have come from the Golden Temple at Amritsar, in Punjab. We are going home now, to Madhya Pradesh. We have long ways still to go."

"Thanks!" I yelled back. "Namaste."

"Namaste," they both said back, as their bus continued moving slowly past me. I looked back down the street behind me again, but still couldn't see the end of the line. There must have been fifty or sixty buses all traveling together. Madhya Pradesh was an Indian state south of Delhi. Although they'd come a long ways from Amritsar, they certainly did have a long ways still to go, especially if they kept this turtle's pace through every little town along the way.

When I finally arrived back at the river near the bustling center of town, the sky was just beginning to dim. The line of buses had slowed to a virtual crawl. I guessed that the people planned to sleep inside them while traveling through the night, since it would clearly be a while before they even made it out of town. At least they had plenty of hands to help share the wheel.

I walked from the street down the crowded steps to the edge of the river, where the evening ceremony was just getting started. Large speakers were placed nearby, blaring Hindi chanting music at almost unbearable levels over the thousands of people gathering at the river's edge. Some of the people talked amongst themselves, some chanted, others simply stared silently into the river. Many of the worshippers held in their hands a small green bowl, made from leaves glued together, then filled with yellow and pink flower petals and with a small candle stuck in the center. I bought one as well for a few rupees from a little girl who came up to me; and then sat down near the river, to wait with everyone else for the designated time of offering.

At one point, darkness having descended, the loud chanting music began to fade and people started taking out matches to light their candles. After lighting them, they began placing the leaf-bowls into the water, to be carried away by the rushing river. Hundreds of these little bowls were placed into the rushing Ganges over the next several minutes. Soon, countless flickering lights floated on top of the water through the darkness. A few tipped over, dousing the flame and spilling the flower petals into the river. A man standing next to me offered some matches so that I could light my own candle. Afterwards, I made a silent prayer and gave thanks for my incredible trip through this profoundly inspiring country, and then set my little bowl into the water as well and watched it bob and float away.

My train to Delhi didn't leave for a couple more hours. But I figured I would head back to the train station and hang out there for the rest of the evening. I felt like I needed to just sit in one spot for a good little while to relax, reflect and calm my nerves, before entering the frenzied activity of Delhi the next morning. I said goodbye to the sacred Ganges and then walked up the stone steps to the busy main street through town. The Sikh bus caravan was still clogging the street, creeping slowly, slowly along. I walked beside it, overtaking it now as I continued back towards the train station, and ultimately back home…

Afterword

...More adventures in wanderlust

I took a break from traveling over the next several years. I arrived back in the United States from India in the spring of 2000, flat broke and, no big surprise, with little idea of what exactly I was doing next. After some concerted pondering, I decided to head in a completely different direction and go back to school to complete my pursuit of a B.A., which I'd abandoned in the mid-'90s, when I left Oregon for a life on the road. Two years later, spring of 2002, I received my B.A. in World Religions from Humboldt State University in northern California.

I moved to Portland, Oregon, where I had some friends from living previously in Oregon, as well as an assortment of family members. I attended a few Rainbow Gatherings during the summers, but didn't do any major trips. I worked for a local delivery service, hiked in the beautiful Cascade mountains, went to hot springs, swam in mountain streams, biked around the city and skied on the side of picturesque Mt. Hood.

Five years after coming back from India, I was ready for more adventure. I made plans to head back to India again for the following winter, for three months. I decided to explore just the south this time, since I would be there through the winter months. I landed in Chennai (formerly Madras), the largest city in Tamil Nadu state, at 11:30 pm on December 31st, 2005, just in time to experience another Indian New Year. This would become an ongoing tradition of sorts over subsequent trips.

Following that trip, I went back to Portland and my old job, and started saving up for something bigger. A year-and-a-half later, I left Portland for an eight-month adventure that would take me to Hawaii, Thailand, India and Nepal. I stopped in Hawaii, on the island of Kauai, both on the way to Asia and on the way back, and both times hiked out to the Kalapani Valley. I spent two-and-a-half months in Thailand, another three months in India, and two weeks in Nepal trekking through the Himalaya to the spectacular Annapurna Base Camp at the base of Mt. Annapurna, tenth highest mountain in the world.

Upon returning from that trip, I decided not to go back to my old job as a delivery driver battling against the frenzied rush hour traffic of the city. Instead, I decided to take advantage of my Canadian heritage. I went on a solo road trip, first to attend the 2008 U.S. national Rainbow Gathering in Wyoming, which happened to be where my first major Rainbow Gathering had been back in 1994. From there I continued driving north into Canada, where I eventually ended up in Jasper National Park, in the Rocky Mountains of Alberta, and found a job working as a gardener for one of the local hotel chains in the small town of Jasper at the center of the park.

After spending the summer in Canada, I decided to head back to Portland, take the old job back and save up some more for another trip. Eight months later, I was stepping onto that big ol' jet airliner once again, this time back to Greece. I took a mountain bike with me, and spent three months exploring Greece, especially the Greek islands, by bike. I met a Greek woman, Dianna, in the course of the trip, who I ended up traveling with for much of the time; and she introduced me to some of the more beautiful Greek islands that most tourists don't make it to, where you could camp on gorgeous beaches for free and enjoy the sand, sun and sea with hardly anyone else around.

I then flew from Greece across the Mediterranean to Egypt for three weeks, where I visited the Great Pyramids and the Valley of the Kings, floated down the Nile and ventured into the vast, desolate deserts of western Egypt. I then flew back to Greece, met up with Dianna and we flew to Turkey for three weeks together.

The highlight of Turkey was, without a doubt, Cappadocia, one of the strangest and most fascinating places I've seen in all of my travels. Bizarre rock formations and "fairy chimneys" (a natural geological phenomenon that looks like massive upside-down ice cream cones) cover a huge area of central Turkey that makes for amazing hiking and exploring. And adding to the intrigue of the region, the area was inhabited for thousands of years by people who carved cave dwellings into the fairy chimneys and cliffs, and even built entire cities completely underground, up to twelve stories deep that could house up to 30,000 people. You can actually take a tour down into one of these underground cities, a complex network of caves and tunnels that feels like something previously inhabited by trolls and goblins, straight out of *Lord of the Rings*.

Following my four months in the Mediterranean, I was back to work in Jasper, Canada, saving up for another trip. Eight months later, in the fall of 2010, I was off yet again, on a five-month trip, this time to the Philippines, Malaysia, Singapore and India for the fourth time (and my fourth Indian New Year's celebration). I went back to Rishikesh on the Ganges, visited the Taj Mahal again, revisited Gokarna where this time I spent two weeks on Om Beach, the beach that I'd visited briefly while searching for the Rainbow Gathering; and I also visited tons of new places, since there's always lots more to see in India. Despite having spent more than fifteen months now traveling around India, I still have a long list of places to see on my next visit.

As for the future, who knows? I'm still living life a day at a time, following the wind, my heart, my gut, my thumb to see what or where I'm meant to explore and experience next. I have a long list of new places I'd love to visit: Spain, where I'd like to walk the Road to Santiago, a popular spiritual pilgrimage route; as well as Australia and New Zealand, Iceland, Mongolia, Mexico, Belize, Peru and Brazil. I hope to go back to Greece to visit other islands that I heard about when I was there, but didn't make it to. And I've also wanted to go back to Egypt, where there is lots more to explore, as well as other parts of the Middle East and North Africa such as Morocco, Tunisia, Jordan, Syria and Israel. But of course, that's very much up in the air for the time being, as political turbulence rocks that part of the world. These days, with so much change going on, you never know where the next revolution or other upheaval is going to spring up.

Life continues to be an adventure in the unknown. I certainly could have planned things out better, put my hard-earned money to more practical things like a down payment on a house. But I don't regret how I've lived my life in the slightest. When it's all said and done, life is simply a series of experiences, which you can grow through and learn something from, if you're lucky. There are a million different ways to approach life, and they each have their own pros and cons, challenges and opportunities. I'm grateful for the chance to have seen some sliver of the rest of the world, how other people live, and to have been challenged by such a wide variety of strange and remarkable experiences. I've missed out on some other valuable experiences in the process. But anytime you make choices, you step through doors as other doors close behind you. So it goes. Perhaps my next two decades won't be quite as exciting and adventurous as the previous twenty years. But I'm happy knowing that I managed to pack a lifetime, or perhaps two, into those years already.

Soul Rocks is a fresh list that takes the search for soul
and spirit mainstream. Chick-lit, young adult, cult,
fashionable fiction & non-fiction with a fierce twist.